VISUAL QUICKSTART GUIDE

AUTOMATOR

FOR MAC OS X 10.6 SNOW LEOPARD

Ben Waldie

D1522865

Peachpit Press

Visual QuickStart Guide
Automator for Mac OS X 10.6 Snow Leopard
Ben Waldie

Peachpit Press
1249 Eighth Street
Berkeley, CA 94710
510/524-2178
510/524-2221 (fax)

Find us on the Web at: www.peachpit.com
To report errors, please send a note to errata@peachpit.com
Peachpit Press is a division of Pearson Education.

Copyright © 2010 by Ben Waldie

Project Editor: Susan Rimerman
Production Editor: Becky Winter
Developmental/copyeditor: Anne Marie Walker
Technical Editor: Mary Norbury
Proofreader: Liz Welch
Indexer: James Minkin
Composition: David Van Ness
Cover Design: Peachpit Press

ISBN-13: 978-0-321-68583-4
ISBN-10:   0-321-68583-0

9 8 7 6 5 4 3 2 1

Printed and bound in the United States of America

Dedication

For Jen, Lizzie, and Maddie. You keep me going, and I couldn't do it without you.

Acknowledgments

I would like to take this opportunity to sincerely thank a number of people who have directly led to and assisted with the creation of this book.

Thanks to my wife, Jen. Without her, many of the things that I set out to accomplish would not be possible.

Thanks to my two beautiful daughters, Lizzie and Maddie, for your love, support, and above all, patience.

Thanks to my editor, Susan Rimerman, for doing a great job managing the production of this book and for everything else she has done along the way.

Thanks to Anne Marie Walker, Mary Norbury, and Liz Welch for their patience, and for consistently providing great feedback.

Thanks to Becca Freed for kick-starting this project and for all of her help with the previous edition.

Thanks to everyone else at Peachpit who contributed to the publication of this book, as well as its previous edition.

Thanks to Sal Soghoian at Apple, who always offers helpful input, suggestions, and information about Automator and AppleScript.

Thanks to the incredibly talented developers at Apple for implementing and keeping alive such amazing Mac automation technologies. Keep up the good work!

Thanks to Tim Davis for giving me the opportunity to learn AppleScript so very many years ago. Without that opportunity, I would not be where I am today.

About the Author

Ben Waldie, president of Automated Workflows, LLC, has developed professional AppleScript, Automator, and workflow solutions for Mac-based businesses across the globe, including Adobe, Apple, CNN, and Microsoft. In addition to the first edition of this book, Ben is the author of *AppleScripting the Finder* and has written for Apple.com, *Macworld*, *MacTech*, and MacScripter.net. Ben also hosts the *Mac Automation Made Simple* video podcast series (Peachpit Press), is author of AppleScript training CDs for the Virtual Training Company, and is a frequent presenter at Macworld and other industry events.

www.automatedworkflows.com

ben@automatedworkflows.com

TABLE OF CONTENTS

BONUS CHAPTERS ON THE COMPANION WEBSITE

Chapter 13: **Workflow Starting Points**

Processing Files and Folders

Processing Music and Audio

Processing Photos and Images

Processing Movies and Video

Processing Text

Processing Web Content

Chapter 14: **Building Advanced Workflows**

Running AppleScript Commands

Running UNIX Commands

Using AppleScript Variables

Using UNIX Variables

Watch Me Do and AppleScript

AppleScripting Automator

Developer-related Actions

Appendix B: **Example Workflows**

Backup Safari Data

Make Dated Subfolder

Clean Up Desktop

Appendix C: **Developer Resources**

Apple Developer Connection

Websites

Apple Mailing Lists

Third-party Mailing Lists and Forums

Books and Tutorials

Action Templates and Example Code

INTRODUCTION

With its knack for reliably automating complex, repetitive tasks, the personal computer was supposed to make life easier. But does yours really, or does it just make *more* work for you? For many, the latter seems to be the case, but it doesn't have to be. Your computer's ability to make your life easier depends on how you use it. If you're like me, you probably use many different software applications during your workday, and you probably find yourself doing the same things over and over again.

Take digital photography, for example. Each time you plug your digital camera into your computer, you need to download the images into a set of folders, import them into a photo catalog, rename them, assign keywords, and more—sounds like a ton of work. Applications such as iPhoto can help tremendously with these tasks by automating much of the process for you. If you look closely at the tasks you do—known as your *workflow*—you will probably see that many are automated by your existing software.

Everything you do on your computer involves software—it provides you with the tools you need to do page layout, image editing, word processing, and more. Sometimes, your software does its job well; however, this isn't always the case. You may need your software to do things it wasn't quite designed to do. Perhaps an application just doesn't automate those time-consuming tasks that you do regularly. Or, you may need a way to move information between multiple applications. If you're a programmer, you can write your own custom software, or you may be able to automate your existing software using something like AppleScript.

But what if you're not a programmer? Well, your wish has been granted! Installed with Mac OS X is Automator, a tool for average folks that has one job: to perform repetitive tasks the way *you* need them done.

About Automator

Automator's user-friendly interface lets anyone create custom automated tasks, whether simple or complex. Within Automator, you'll work with two main types of components: *actions* and *workflows* (**Figure i.1**).

Figure i.1 Say hello to Automator's friendly little icon mascot, Otto.

◆ Actions are built by developers and are installed onto your Mac either individually or with an application. Each action's responsibility is to perform a single specific task, such as opening a file, checking for new email, or rotating an image.

◆ Workflows are designed and built by you: You place a series of actions to create an assembly line of tasks. You can save workflows and run them later in a variety of ways, such as from within Automator, from the Mac OS X Finder, from iCal, and more.

Programmers are in luck, too: Mac OS X includes all the tools necessary to build custom actions. You plug them right into Automator to extend your automation possibilities even further.

Benefits of Automator

Automator is much easier to use than any automation technology that's been available before and includes many of the same benefits. After you've created a few workflows, you'll wonder how you ever functioned without Automator. Its main benefits include:

◆ **Ease of use.** Automator's simple user interface makes automation easy for anyone with a decent grasp of how to get around Mac OS X. With Automator, it doesn't take a rocket scientist (or a skilled programmer) to build an automated workflow. By putting such an easy-to-use tool directly into the hands of a typical Mac user, Apple ensures that anyone can take advantage of automation.

◆ **Less stress.** Automator can actually reduce stress. That's right, you read that correctly. Automator reduces stress. By removing the same old repetitive, boring tasks from your workload, you'll feel a renewed sense of energy and motivation as you become free to focus on things that you actually enjoy, such as graphic design, photography, and more. Spend your time being more creative.

◆ **Fewer mistakes.** No matter what we might like to think, we all make mistakes from time to time—entering an incorrect filename, accidentally deleting a file, moving a file into the wrong folder, and so on. By automating tasks, you can eliminate these sorts of mistakes. A properly created Automator workflow doesn't make mistakes. It performs consistently and accurately day in and day out, like a robot.

◆ **Do more faster!** An Automator workflow interacts directly with your Mac, eliminating time spent moving and clicking the mouse, pressing keys on the keyboard, and mulling over what to do next. Thus, you accomplish more work in the same amount of time. In some cases, it may even be possible for your workflow to run while you're away from your computer—at lunch or when you leave at the end of a day.

What Can Automator Do for You?

This will vary, depending on your specific workflow needs. Every Mac user's workflow is different, and every Automator workflow you build will be different.

Here are a few of the tasks Automator can do:

◆ **File and folder processing.** Quickly create workflows that rename files and folders on your Mac, compress them into archives, burn them to disc, and more.

◆ **Music- and audio-related tasks.** Build a workflow that simply plays music in iTunes. Or, create a more involved workflow that downloads songs from a website, imports them into iTunes, and syncs them with your iPod.

◆ **Photo and image conversion and manipulation.** If you're like me, you probably have thousands of digital photos and images on your Mac. Don't work with them one at a time. Instead, create workflows that batch process photos and images, converting them from one format

to another. Quickly and easily manipulate them with workflows that perform scaling, cropping, rotating, and more.

◆ **PDF processing.** Need to encrypt a PDF, add a watermark, or insert metadata? Built-in PDF actions make it easy to create workflows to batch process your PDF documents.

◆ **Email- and Internet-related tasks.** Create Automator workflows that download photos from Web pages and import them into iPhoto, or upload files to your website, email files, and more.

◆ **Folder watching.** Create a workflow that watches a folder on your Mac. Simply drop files into that folder to run the workflow, allowing the files to be processed.

◆ **Scheduled workflows.** Use iCal to schedule workflows to run anytime—even if you're in a meeting or it's the middle of the night!

◆ **System-wide processing.** Save workflows into the Mac OS X *Services* menu, which gives you quick access to process files, text, URLs, and more in virtually any application.

What Can't Automator Do for You?

Automator can do a lot, but it can't do everything. Like all good software, it still has limitations:

◆ **Automator can't make decisions.** It can do only the things you tell it to do, exactly the way you specify, in the order that you specify. It can't choose different courses of action based on varying conditions, which more advanced automation technologies (such as AppleScript) can.

◆ **In Snow Leopard, you can create an Automator workflow that runs repeatedly (or *loops*). But information is still passed through the workflow in a linear fashion.** In other words, there's no built-in way to have Automator pass one file at a time through the workflow. For example, let's say you create a workflow that performs three tasks: open a file, make a change, and save the file. If you are processing 700 files, all 700 files will be opened first, then all 700 files will have a change made, then all 700 files will be saved. This can really make processing large numbers of files difficult because you probably don't want 700 files open at once on your desktop.

✔ Tips

■ Chapter 7, "Workflow Looping," discusses some ways to get around Automator's linear processing limitation. One way is to download my Automator Multi-Item Processing Utility from www. automatedworkflows.com/software/ automator_actions/automator_tools. html. This free tool converts Automator workflows to AppleScript applications. After converting the workflow, simply drag and drop multiple files or folders onto the AppleScript application to process them one at a time through the workflow.

■ If you occasionally feel limited by the actions available to you, just look around because the list is still growing. In addition to the dozens of Automator actions Apple provides in Mac OS X, more are included with specific Apple applications, such as iPhoto and Keynote, as well as some popular third-party applications like Microsoft Word and Excel. Additional actions are also being released regularly by third-party developers. Visit www.apple.com/downloads/macosx/ automator to see what's available.

When to Use AppleScript

Need to do something Automator can't handle? Try AppleScript. Though it has a much steeper learning curve than Automator, it too can be self-taught. I know because I taught myself AppleScript.

With a little time and practice, you can write AppleScripts to automate virtually any task in Mac OS X. As you'll learn in Bonus Chapter 14, "Building Advanced Workflows," available online, AppleScripts can even be plugged into your Automator workflows to extend Automator's reach.

No time to learn a scripting language? Prewritten AppleScripts are a good introduction, and you can find plenty of them online. Visit www.macosxautomation.com to get started.

System Requirements

Automator was first released with Mac OS X 10.4 (Tiger), which is the minimum installation to use Automator. Mac OS X 10.5 (Leopard) introduced a completely revamped version of Automator with loads of new useful features and a redesigned interface. Mac OS X 10.6 (Snow Leopard) continues to build on Leopard's enhancements with even more features designed to make Automator easier to use and more useful than ever.

This book focuses on using Automator in Snow Leopard and with the applications installed with Mac OS X. While some of the main principles and topics will still be pertinent to Tiger and Leopard users, many discussions will be Snow Leopard specific.

Likewise, some of the example workflows provided involve iLife and iWork applications, such as iPhoto or Keynote. If you don't have these installed, simply do your best to follow along.

Figure i.2 Automator's interface in Snow Leopard is improved and much quicker than in Tiger.

Figure i.3 Inserting audio, photos, and movies into a workflow is a snap with Automator's Media Browser.

Figure i.4 Automator can watch your every move. Record your mouse clicks and keystrokes, and play them back as part of a workflow.

New with Automator in Snow Leopard?

Automator was off to a great start in Tiger, but it was still a 1.0 release. Mac OS X 10.5 Leopard was a giant leap forward, introducing a number of enhancements, including:

◆ **Revamped interface.** A slick new interface emerges that's easier to use and customize (**Figure i.2**).

◆ **Better performance.** There's no way around it, building Automator workflows in Tiger was a sluggish process. Automator's interface becomes quick and snappy, allowing you to build and edit workflows in a flash.

◆ **Media Browser.** Automator makes it easy to quickly insert audio, photos, and music into a workflow with just a few clicks of the mouse (**Figure i.3**).

◆ **Recording.** Use Automator to control almost any Mac OS X application. Simply tell Automator to watch your mouse clicks and keystrokes, and then play them back as part of a workflow (**Figure i.4**).

◆ **Variables.** One of the most useful additions, variables, allows you to store information at one point in a workflow and refer back to it at a later time. Variables can also be used to integrate dynamic content, such as dates, information about the current user, and more into your workflows.

Mac OS X 10.6 Snow Leopard continues to build upon Leopard's improvements, taking Automator to the next level. New Automator features in Snow Leopard include:

◆ **Workflow templates.** Creating workflows has never been easier. Automator now helps get you started by prompting you up front to choose the type of workflow you want to create. Options include Application, Service, Folder Action, iCal Alarm, Print Plugin, and more (**Figure i.5**).

◆ **Services.** Perhaps the most exciting new Automator feature in Snow Leopard is the ability to save workflows as services. A service is a type of plug-in, which can be run from a system-wide *Services* menu and certain applications' contextual menus in Mac OS X. In the past, Automator allowed users to run workflows from the Finder's contextual menu to process selected files and folders. Workflows saved as services, however, can be run from within virtually *any* application and can process a variety of types of input, such as selected text, image files, email addresses, or URLs, providing even greater flexibility and extensibility.

Figure i.5 Automator's templates allow you to choose the type of workflow you want to build.

◆ **More reliable folder action workflows.**
Automator has always allowed you to
save a workflow as a folder action, that is,
a workflow that will run whenever items
are added to an attached folder (think hot
folder/watched folder). Unfortunately,
folder action workflows have had a
knack for being a tad unreliable. Snow
Leopard, however, introduces some key
improvements. For one, the folder actions
background application in Mac OS X now
runs Automator workflows directly. In
the past, an intermediate AppleScript file
was used to run the workflow, thus adding a potential point of failure. Another
welcome enhancement is that folder
actions now attempt to wait for items
to be written before processing them. In
the past, workflows had a tendency to
begin running while items were still being
copied or saved, thus usually causing the
workflow to fail.

◆ **Improved actions.** A number of
actions in Snow Leopard have also been
improved. In particular, you'll see a lot
of changes in the *Filter* and *Find* actions,
which are generally more reliable and have
a variety of new options. For example, the
Filter Finder Items action now allows you
to filter files by size, modification date,
and label color—no doubt welcome additions for many Automator users.

NEW WITH AUTOMATOR IN SNOW LEOPARD?

About This Book

Automator for Mac OS X 10.6 Snow Leopard: Visual QuickStart Guide is written for any Mac enthusiast interested in learning how to use Automator regardless of skill level. Whether a beginner or an expert, you'll find that this book covers Automator from top to bottom.

While you're certainly free to skip around, the chapters are arranged in a logical manner. For the best possible learning experience, move through them in order.

If you do, you'll begin by exploring some of Automator's key concepts that you'll use throughout the book.

Next, you'll create some simple Automator workflows. Hands-on experience is perhaps the best way to learn Automator. These workflows are designed to familiarize you with Automator's interface and help Automator's key concepts to sink in.

The remainder of the book covers Automator in detail. Screen shots and step-by-step instructions carefully walk you through all aspects of Automator, including creating, saving, and running workflows, and much more. You'll be up and running with Automator in no time!

Bonus Chapters and Content

There's a lot to cover when it comes to Automator. We've created additional bonus chapters on "Workflow Starting Points" and "Building Advanced Workflows" available online. Also two more appendices on "Example Workflows" and "Developer Resources." You will also find completed versions of all the example workflows discussed throughout this text.

To access this material, follow this link to the Automator site at: www.peachpit.com/vqs/automator-snow-leopard. You will need to register your book by creating a Peachpit login account, entering the book ISBN code (0321685830), and answering a security question (answer found in the book). Look for the link "access to protected content" on the book page after you register.

GETTING STARTED

1

Automator's purpose is to help you to become more efficient. It works with the files, folders, applications, and the operating system on your Mac to automate time-consuming or repetitive tasks. When using Automator, you'll first think about an overall job you want to accomplish. Next, you'll identify the applications or processes that will be involved, and finally, you'll specify the individual tasks you want to perform within those applications or processes.

In Automator, each task is called an *action*, and you can link multiple actions together to form a *workflow*. The workflow you create can run within Automator, or you can save it to run outside of Automator in a variety of ways. When run, the actions within your workflow execute sequentially, in some cases passing information between one another.

For example, you might create a workflow that retrieves unread emails from your inbox, converts them to audio format, adds them to iTunes, and syncs them with your iPod, allowing you to listen to your email on the go. You'll soon find that Automator makes it easy to create useful workflows for photos, music, text, and more.

About Workflows

Automator documents are called *workflows*.
You build a workflow by gathering and configuring the actions for the tasks you want to
automate. You can then perform these tasks
at any time simply by running the workflow.

✔ Tips

■ Look for example workflows to get
you started. A good online source is
www.apple.com/downloads/macosx/
automator, or you can try other third-
party Automator sites.

■ Don't be afraid to use or build onto
another person's existing workflow.

■ Be sure to spread the good word about
Automator. Share your own workflows
with others, too.

You can run workflows in a variety of ways:

◆ From within Automator

◆ As applications from outside of Automator

◆ As plugins for other applications or processes

✔ Tips

■ If desired, you can schedule workflows to
run at a specific time, such as in the middle of the night or while you're at lunch.

■ A workflow can be attached to a folder, so
it will run automatically when new files
are added to the folder.

■ Workflows can be configured to process
selected text, URLs, or other content
within applications.

■ You can add workflow applications as
login items, allowing them to run automatically whenever you log into your
machine.

About Actions

Most Automator actions are designed to perform a single specific task, such as writing text to a file, opening a URL, or copying files from one location to another. In some cases, a single action may do everything that you need. You also can link Automator actions sequentially, however, to form a larger, more complex, multipart, automated process, such as downloading songs from a website, importing them into iTunes, and syncing them with your iPod.

Determine the actions to use

Before building a workflow, you need to figure out what you want to automate. Look for tasks you do manually that take a lot of time or are repetitive. For example, renaming and resizing image files are both time-consuming and repetitive. Now look for actions that can do these things for you. To get started:

◆ Think of the tasks that you normally need to perform manually.

◆ Think of each step in your manual workflow as a single Automator action.

When you build your workflow in Automator, you'll assemble these actions together to form your complete workflow.

✔ Tips

■ Try outlining your desired workflow. It's a good idea to step through the sequence of manual tasks, and outline each step as you go.

■ Think about how you want to run your completed workflow—for example, as a stand-alone application or from within another application—perhaps to process selected text. Thinking this through up front will help you to identify the type of workflow to create. It will also dictate some of the actions you may need to include at the beginning of the workflow.

■ Need to create a repeating workflow? Learn how to use Automator's Loop action in Chapter 7, "Workflow Looping."

Action input and output

In a workflow, an action can get information (input) from the previous action, and pass information (output) down to the next action. For example, you can build a workflow that retrieves photos from a folder, compresses them into an archive, and attaches the archive to a new email message. You would need four Automator actions for this:

1. **Ask for Finder Items (Figure 1.1).** Asks the user to choose a folder of photos. It then passes that folder down (output) to the next action (input) in the workflow.

2. **Get Folder Contents (Figure 1.2).** Gets a list of any files in the folder passed as input and passes those files to the next action in the workflow.

3. **Create Archive (Figure 1.3).** Compresses the list of files passed from the previous action into a zip archive. The location of the created archive is then passed to the final action in the workflow.

4. **New Mail Message (Figure 1.4).** Tells Mail to create a new email message and attaches the archive passed from the previous action.

Actions can pass a variety of information between one another, such as file and folder paths, text, email messages, and so forth. The task an action performs determines the type of information it inputs or outputs.

✔ Tip

■ Not all actions accept input or pass output; whether they do or not depends on their function.

Figure 1.1 The Ask for Finder Items action asks the user to choose a folder of photos.

Figure 1.2 The Get Folder Contents action gets a list of any files in the folder that was passed from the previous action.

Figure 1.3 The Create Archive action builds a zip archive containing the files passed from the previous action.

Figure 1.4 The New Mail Message action creates a new email and attaches the archive passed from the previous action.

Figure 1.5 The Download URLs action accepts URLs as input but passes files and folders as its result.

Some actions accept one kind of information as input but output a different kind. For example, the Download URLs action, included with Automator, accepts a list of URLs from a previous action as its input (**Figure 1.5**). It then downloads the specified URLs and outputs the file paths of the downloaded files to the next action for further processing.

Many actions are designed to process information passed to them by the previous action. When adding actions to a workflow, therefore, take care that each action passes the right kind of information to the next one in a workflow. For example, an action that compresses files into a zip archive can accept only file paths as input from the previous action. Passing the wrong kind of information to an action produces an error, or the action simply ignores the information and does nothing. Chapter 4, "Working with Actions," provides more detail on adding actions into workflows.

✔ Tips

- Just passing through? Some actions don't generate output of their own. Instead, they pass their input down as output for further processing.

- Check an action's description area to see the kinds of input and output it uses.

ABOUT ACTIONS

Conversion Actions

Sometimes you may need to put two actions together whose output and input don't match. In these situations, Automator will try to convert the mismatched output from the first action to the right kind of input for the second.

To do this, Automator uses *conversion actions*. Conversion actions are built into Mac OS X but aren't visible within Automator's interface. You don't need to worry about adding conversion actions into a workflow. Automator automatically does this in the background when the workflow runs.

Whenever Automator finds mismatched actions together, it looks for a conversion action that can change the first action's output to the correct input type for the next action in the workflow. If it finds a conversion action, the workflow runs successfully. Because conversion actions are not visible within Automator's interface, you probably won't even know that this process has happened. If Automator can't find a conversion action, it may return an error when the workflow runs, or the second action may ignore the output of the first action.

Figure 1.6 shows an example of mismatched output/input values. The Get Selected iTunes Items action (shown as Get Selected iTunes Tracks because it's configured to get selected tracks) retrieves a list of any selected tracks in iTunes and passes them to the Copy Finder Items action. The Copy Finder Items action accepts files and folders as its input, however, not iTunes items. When you run this workflow, Automator runs a conversion action behind the scenes to convert the iTunes items to Files/Folders, so that they can be processed without a problem.

Automator's log area, covered later in this chapter, will show you where conversions are used when your workflow runs (**Figure 1.7**).

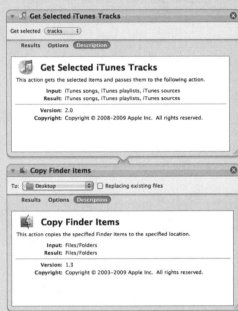

Figure 1.6 Mismatched action output/input. The result of the Get Selected iTunes Items action is iTunes items, but the input for the Copy Finder Items action is Files/Folders. This is handled behind the scenes by a conversion action.

Conversion Action

Figure 1.7 Automator's log indicates when conversion actions run.

Settings

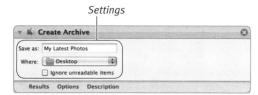

Figure 1.8 The Create Archive action has modifiable settings, including the name and save location for the archive.

Figure 1.9 The Update iPod action has no modifiable settings.

Action settings

Actions don't always know exactly what you want them to do. Sometimes you may need to tell them how to behave by specifying certain details, such as where to save a file, what name to use, and so forth.

As Chapter 4 details, when you build a workflow, you often have the ability to specify settings for actions. These settings control how the action behaves when the workflow runs.

Remember the workflow that compresses photos into a zip archive and then attaches the archive to a new email message in Mail? Several of its actions have modifiable settings.

For example, the Create Archive action allows you to specify a name (*My Latest Photos*) and output folder (*Desktop*) for the archive, and whether any unreadable items should be ignored (**Figure 1.8**).

Some actions perform a single, very basic task and may not require settings to be specified at all. For example, Automator includes an iTunes action for updating a connected iPod (**Figure 1.9**). This action doesn't require any settings to be specified. It simply uses iTunes to update any connected iPod.

✔ Tip

■ If you're unsure of what an action's setting does, check its description for more information, or see if it has any accompanying documentation.

ABOUT ACTIONS

Action options

In some cases, you may not want to configure an action's settings when you build the workflow. Instead, you may want the action's settings to be specified when the workflow runs.

To allow for this, many actions can be configured to display their settings when the workflow runs. For example, you may decide that you want to change the name of the zip archive occasionally in the photo compression workflow. To do this, you can configure the Create Archive action to display when the workflow runs (**Figures 1.10** and **1.11**).

✔ Tips

- Allow for customization. Others may want or need a workflow to run differently than you do. If you plan to share your workflow with others, consider configuring some actions in the workflow to display when run.

- Some actions can be configured to show only specified settings rather than all settings, allowing you to pick and choose which settings will be modifiable when the workflow runs (**Figures 1.12** and **1.13**).

Show action when run

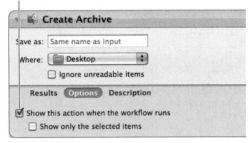

Figure 1.10 Configuring the Create Archive action to display when run.

Figure 1.11 The Create Archive action as it appears when run.

Selected items   *Show only selected items*

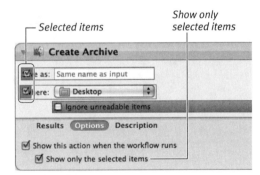

Figure 1.12 Configuring the Create Archive action to display only selected settings when run.

Figure 1.13 The Create Archive action, displaying only selected settings when run.

Figure 1.14 The New Folder action builds a folder named *Website Photos* on the desktop.

Variable

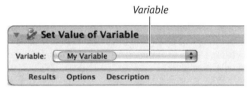

Figure 1.15 The Set Value of Variable action stores the Website Photos folder created by the previous action for reference later in the workflow.

About Variables

An action in a workflow can receive information from the previous action, and it can pass information down to the next action. But what about two actions that don't appear together in a workflow? Can they still share information with one another? The answer is yes! Automator includes a powerful feature called *variables* that can help you create robust workflows. Variables allow you to store information, such as File/Folder references or text, in memory at a certain point in a workflow and refer back to it at a later time.

For example, suppose you want to build a workflow that creates a folder on the desktop, gets the current webpage in Safari, retrieves the URLs of images linked from that page, and then downloads those URLs into the newly created folder. In this workflow, the first action would create the folder, and the last action would download URLs into that folder. Several other actions fall between these two, however, so how will the last action know about the folder created by the first? The solution is to use a variable to store the folder when the first action creates it. The last action can then reference this variable when it needs to access the folder. The final workflow consists of these five actions:

1. **New Folder (Figure 1.14).** This action creates a folder named *Website Photos* on the desktop, if one does not already exist. It passes a reference to the newly created folder to the next action in the workflow.

2. **Set Value of Variable (Figure 1.15).** This action accepts the reference to the folder from the previous action, and stores it in a variable named *My Variable* for future reference. (Chapter 8, "Using Variables," covers naming and using variables in detail.)

continues on next page

ABOUT VARIABLES

3. **Get Current Webpage from Safari (Figure 1.16).** This action ignores the results of the previous action, gets the current webpage from Safari, and passes it down to the next action in the workflow.

4. **Get Image URLs from Webpage (Figure 1.17).** This action locates the URLs of any image links on the webpage passed from the previous action and outputs these URLs to the next action in the workflow.

5. **Download URLs (Figure 1.18).** This action downloads the image URLs passed from the previous action. The problem is that this action received only the image URLs as input. It doesn't know about the folder that was created at the start of the workflow. To work around this issue, you can refer back to the variable *My Variable*.

✔ Tips

■ Want to test the preceding workflow? Try replicating the actions and settings in the screen shots. Then open this sample photo webpage in Safari and run the workflow— www.automatedworkflows.com/demos/ photos.

■ Sorry Tiger users. Variables didn't debut in Automator until Mac OS X 10.5 Leopard.

Preexisting variables

You can also retrieve values from a number of built-in, preexisting variables that can dynamically provide dates, times, locations, system information, user information, and more to your workflow at runtime. For example, you might want the name of that new photos folder to include the name of the current weekday. You could add it by referencing Automator's built-in Current weekday variable in the New Folder action's Name field (**Figures 1.19** and **1.20**). Chapter 8 explores preexisting variables, as well as how to add variables into actions and workflows.

Figure 1.16 The Get Current Webpage from Safari action gets the currently opened webpage in Safari.

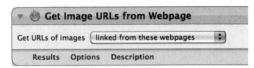

Figure 1.17 The Get Image URLs from Webpage action retrieves URLs to any images in the webpage from the previous action.

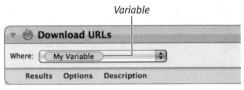

Figure 1.18 The Download URLs action downloads the image URLs from the previous action into the stored Website Photos folder.

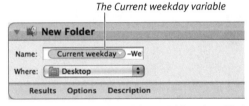

Figure 1.19 The Current weekday variable to be added to the name of a new folder.

Friday–Website Photos

Figure 1.20
A new folder named with the current weekday.

✔ Tip

■ If variables seem confusing, don't feel like you need to start using them right away. Get comfortable creating workflows first, and then move on to variables.

Which Applications Work with Automator?

To control an application with Automator, you must have actions for that application installed on your Mac. Many times, these actions are built right into the application or installed automatically, but sometimes you must manually install them separately. To get you started, Mac OS X includes hundreds of actions that cover most of the core Apple applications, including Address Book, the Finder, iTunes, Mail, and Safari, as well as application-independent activities, such as manipulating images, setting the audio volume on your system, or taking a screen shot.

As you install other Apple software, you may also begin to see more actions appearing in Automator. For example, iLife automatically adds actions for iPhoto and iDVD.

✔ Tip

■ Automator actions are installed with a number of other Apple applications, including Aperture, Keynote, Apple Remote Desktop, and Soundtrack Pro.

Some non-Apple applications also now have built-in actions that automatically appear in Automator when you install the application. In addition, loads of third-party developers are releasing Automator actions for a variety of applications and processes.

BBEdit was the first commercial application with built-in Automator actions, and the list is growing. Third-party applications with built-in Automator actions now include Fetch, GraphicConverter, Microsoft Office 2008, NetNewsWire, Stuffit Deluxe, and Transmit.

Some third-party applications are bundled with Automator actions that need to be installed separately.

Third-party developers have also released Automator actions for applications including Adobe Illustrator, Adobe InDesign, Adobe Photoshop, FileMaker Pro, iView MediaPro, and QuarkXPress.

✔ Tips

- For a comprehensive, up-to-date list of third-party Automator actions, visit Apple's Mac OS X download website at www.apple.com/downloads/macosx/automator/, or check out www.automatoractions.com.

- Having trouble finding actions for an application? Consider contacting the application developer. Make it known that you want Automator actions for the application and provide some ideas of what you want to do with those actions.

- You may still be able to control an application with Automator even if it doesn't have actions of its own. As you'll learn in Chapter 6, "Recording Manual Events," Automator now supports recording your manual tasks in lots of Mac OS X applications.

- Are you an AppleScripter? If so, you can create your own Automator actions for any AppleScriptable application using Xcode. Bonus Appendix C, available online (see Introduction), will give you the details.

Figure 1.21 Automator's interface may seem complex at first, but you'll soon find that it's fairly straightforward.

Getting to Know Automator's Interface

So far, we've explored some of the key concepts of Automator, including actions, workflows, and variables. Now let's dive in a bit deeper to see how the components of its interface come together. Automator's interface may seem complex at first glance (**Figure 1.21**). Once you get to know it, however, you'll find it fairly simple and straightforward to navigate. Here's a look at Automator's primary parts.

✔ Tips

- Don't expect to catch on to Automator's interface instantly. To learn your way around, build a few basic workflows. Things will start to fall into place and make sense with time.

- You can customize many aspects of Automator's interface, hiding some areas, resizing others, and so forth. Chapter 10, "Customizing Automator," explores this further.

Understanding workflow templates

When you first launch Automator, a new workflow window opens with a templates panel attached. New to Automator in Snow Leopard, this panel (**Figure 1.22**) makes it easy to begin building workflows. Simply choose the type of workflow you want to create, and Automator will open the appropriate template to get you started. Then you can dive right in and begin adding actions to the workflow. When you save the workflow, depending on the chosen template, Automator will even handle saving it into the proper location on your Mac and enabling it for use.

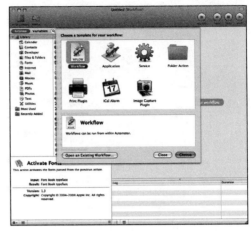

Figure 1.22 The templates panel attached to a workflow window.

✔ Tips

- Some workflow templates provide options that allow you to control the kind of information the workflow can process.

- In Leopard, workflow templates were a bit different. A Starting Points panel allowed you to choose the kind of information the workflow should process. Options included Files & Folders, Music & Audio, Photos & Images, and Text. Automator then created a workflow, inserting some initial actions to retrieve the specified information. You then built upon the initial actions to form your workflow and saved it in the desired format.

- Workflow templates and Starting Points didn't exist for Automator in Tiger. If you're a Tiger user, you'll have to create all your workflows from scratch, and then save them in the appropriate format.

GETTING TO KNOW AUTOMATOR'S INTERFACE

Figure 1.23 Running a service workflow from an application's main menu.

Figure 1.24 Running a service workflow from an application's contextual menu.

In Snow Leopard, Automator includes the following types of workflow templates:

◆ **Workflow.** A file that can be opened and run within Automator or resaved as an application. Some external applications and processes can run workflow files, including Microsoft Word 2008 and the system-wide script menu.

◆ **Application.** Works like any other application in Mac OS X. Double-click it in the Finder to run it, add it to your Dock for quick access, or drop files or folders onto it to begin processing them. Workflow applications can also be opened in Automator and resaved as workflow files.

◆ **Service.** As a plugin for the Mac OS X services architecture, a service workflow can be enabled for a specific application or for all the applications on your Mac. Once enabled, you can run the workflow by selecting it from the Services menu in the application's main menu (**Figure 1.23**). In some cases, you can even run service workflows from contextual menus to process selected text, URLs, image files, and more (**Figure 1.24**).

◆ **Folder Action.** Used to create custom watched folders. When attached to any folder on your Mac, the workflow will automatically run whenever files are placed into the folder. For example, you could set up a folder action workflow that notifies you whenever a file is added to your home folder's public drop box.

continues on next page

GETTING TO KNOW AUTOMATOR'S INTERFACE

◆ **Print Plugin.** The workflow appears in the Print window's PDF pop-up menu (**Figure 1.25**). When run, the current document is printed to PDF and then passed to the workflow for processing. Print plugins provide a way for you to customize Mac OS X's built in print-to-PDF behavior with workflows that automatically encrypt, back up, and upload printed PDFs, and more.

◆ **iCal Alarm.** The workflow is run by an iCal event alarm at a scheduled time. Save time by setting up workflows that run at night, on the weekend, or whenever you have downtime.

◆ **Image Capture Plugin.** The workflow can be run as an automatic task when downloading images from your digital camera with Image Capture. Create advanced photo workflows that add Spotlight comments to your photos, back them up, import them into iPhoto, and more, all while downloading them from your camera (**Figure 1.26**).

Chapter 5, "Types of Workflows," will walk you through all the types of workflows that you can create using Automator's workflow templates.

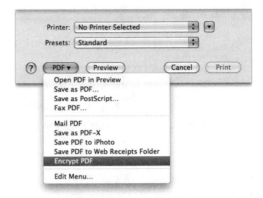

Figure 1.25 Running a print plugin workflow from the Mac OS X print window.

Figure 1.26 Running a plugin workflow in Image Capture.

Understanding Automator's toolbar

The toolbar at the top of an Automator workflow window gives you quick access to common functions (**Figure 1.27**). Just click a button to begin recording manual tasks, run a workflow, or open Automator's Media Browser to access your music, photos, and movies. As you'll learn in Chapter 10, the buttons in the toolbar can be customized as well.

✔ Tip

■ Can't find an action to do what you need? Click the Record button in Automator's toolbar to begin recording manual tasks within an application, such as selecting menus, clicking buttons, and typing text. You can then play those tasks back as part of your workflow.

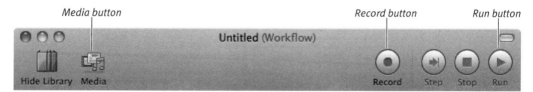

Media button   *Record button*   *Run button*

Figure 1.27 Automator's toolbar.

Understanding Automator's Media Browser

Often, you may want to create a workflow that processes music, photos, or movies. Automator's Media Browser allows you to preview and navigate these items visually. To process an item, simply drag it from the Media Browser into a workflow (**Figure 1.28**).

To display Automator's Media Browser:

Click the Media button in the workflow window's toolbar (**Figure 1.29**).

or

Choose Window > Media Browser (**Figure 1.30**).

The Media Browser is displayed.

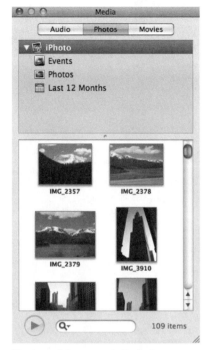

Figure 1.28 Automator's Media Browser window.

Figure 1.29 Clicking the Media button in the workflow window's toolbar displays the Media Browser.

Figure 1.30 Choosing to display Automator's Media Browser window.

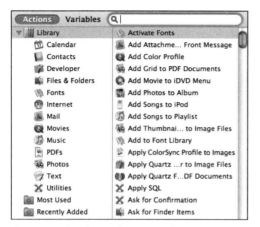

Figure 1.31 The Library of actions and variables in an Automator workflow window.

Understanding the Actions and Variables Library

The left side of the workflow window contains a library of available actions and variables (**Figure 1.31**). The Library is split into two columns:

◆ **Categories/Applications.** This column lists the categories or applications of actions or variables.

◆ **Actions/Variables.** This column lists the actions or variables within the selected category or application.

You select actions and variables within the Library list and drag them into a workflow area to form an Automator workflow. As you install more Automator-ready applications, or third-party actions, the list of available actions will expand.

To view a list of available actions:

Click the Actions button at the top of the Library area to display a list of action categories in the Library's left column (**Figure 1.32**).

By default, Automator's actions are arranged in categories such as:

◆ **Calendar.** Actions for performing calendar-related tasks in such applications as iCal.

◆ **Files & Folders.** Actions for copying, moving, compressing, and otherwise manipulating files and folders.

◆ **Internet.** Actions for downloading and opening URLs in Safari, as well as other Internet-related operations.

◆ **Mail.** Actions for creating emails, opening emails, and more.

◆ **Movies.** Actions for working with movies in DVD Player, QuickTime, and similar applications.

◆ **Music.** Actions for importing audio files into iTunes, syncing your iPod, and more.

◆ **Photos.** Actions for resizing or cropping images, importing images into iPhoto, and more.

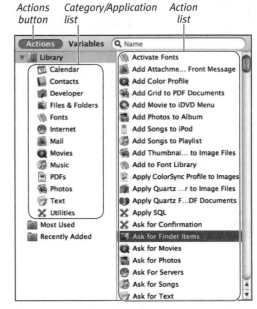

Actions button *Category/Application list* *Action list*

Figure 1.32 The Library list of actions, arranged by category.

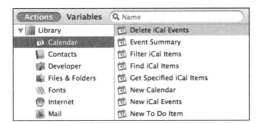

Figure 1.33 Viewing the Calendar category of actions.

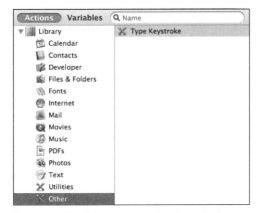

Figure 1.34 The Other category of actions, displaying a third-party action that doesn't fit into a built-in category.

To view the actions within a category:

Click the category name in the left column of the Library list to display the actions within that category in the right column (**Figure 1.33**).

✔ Tip

- If you have actions installed that don't fall into one of Automator's built-in categories, look for them in the Other category, which appears at the bottom of the Library list (**Figure 1.34**). If you don't see this category, all of your installed actions fit into Automator's built-in categories.

To view all actions:

Click the Library item at the top of the left column of the Library list to display a list of actions for all categories (**Figure 1.35**).

In Tiger, actions were arranged by application only. If you would feel more comfortable with this familiar view, you can arrange the action list by application rather than by category (**Figure 1.36**).

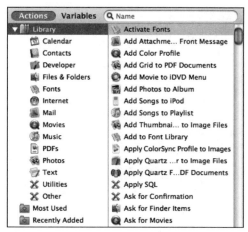

Figure 1.35 Viewing a list of all installed actions.

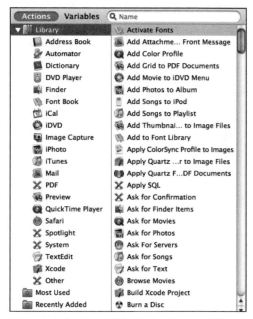

Figure 1.36 The Library list of actions, arranged by application.

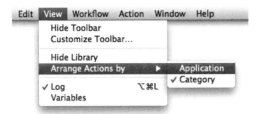

Figure 1.37 Arranging actions by application rather than by category.

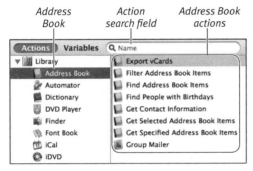

Figure 1.38 Viewing actions by application.

To arrange actions by application:

Choose View > Arrange Actions by > Application (**Figure 1.37**).

✔ Tips

- Automator remembers your view choices. If you configure Automator to arrange actions by application, actions will still be arranged that way the next time Automator launches.

- When you view actions by application, some actions remain listed in categories, such as PDF and System. These categories are used to organize actions that aren't tied to a specific application.

- Some actions may be listed in multiple applications or categories.

To view the actions associated with an application:

Click the application name in the Library list to display a list of actions for that application (**Figure 1.38**).

✔ Tips

- Need to quickly locate an action? Type its name or a related keyword into the Search field at the top of the Library area (Figure 1.38).

- As you'll learn in Chapter 10, you can create your own custom groupings of commonly used actions in Automator's Library list.

GETTING TO KNOW AUTOMATOR'S INTERFACE

To view a list of available variables:

Just as you can choose how the Library list displays actions, you can instruct it to display a list of Automator's predefined variables.

Click the Variables button at the top of the Library area to display a list of variables (**Figure 1.39**).

Variables in the Library list are arranged into several categories:

◆ **Date & Time.** Variables relating to dates and times, such as the current date.

◆ **Locations.** Variables for various locations on your Mac, such as your Movies or Photos folder.

◆ **System.** Variables for such system information as your IP address or operating system version.

◆ **Text & Data.** Variables for storing text content and other kinds of data.

◆ **User.** Variables for user-specific information, such as your first or last name, email address, or phone number.

◆ **Utilities.** Advanced AppleScript and shell script variables, and variables for getting random numbers and identifiers.

To view the variables within a category:

Click the category name in the Library list (**Figure 1.40**).

Variables button

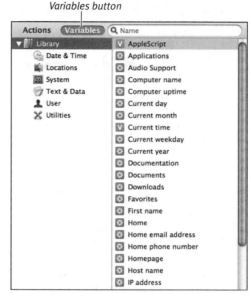

Figure 1.39 Viewing workflow variables.

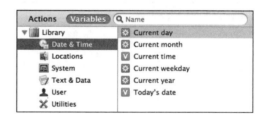

Figure 1.40 Viewing a category of variables.

GETTING TO KNOW AUTOMATOR'S INTERFACE

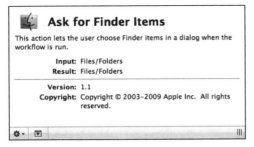

Figure 1.41 The description of the Ask for Finder Items action.

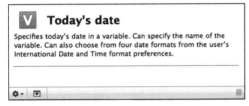

Figure 1.42 The description for the Today's date variable.

Viewing the action and variable description area

When you select an action or variable in the Library, Automator displays its description in the bottom-left corner of the workflow window (**Figures 1.41** and **1.42**).

Action descriptions vary in length and content. Some are highly descriptive, but others may contain little information or be extremely confusing.

Action descriptions may include:

◆ An overview of the action's functionality

◆ A list of input and output types for the action

◆ A list of other related actions

◆ A link to the developer's website

◆ Alerts

◆ Copyright notices

◆ Notes

◆ Options

◆ Requirements

✔ Tips

■ If you don't know what an action does, consult its description for more information.

■ Some third-party actions may have accompanying documentation or example workflows, which can provide you with more information about the action's behavior.

Understanding the workflow area

You've made it! The main part of an Automator workflow window is the workflow area (**Figure 1.43**). This is where you'll spend most of your time. To create a workflow, simply drag one or more actions from the Library list into the workflow area. A detailed view of the added action appears, giving you access to the action's settings and options. Within the workflow area, actions can be configured, rearranged, disabled, and more.

Viewing the workflow status area

When you run a workflow within Automator, the bottom of the workflow window provides brief status messages that tell you which action in the workflow is currently running (**Figure 1.44**). When a workflow finishes, the status area tells you if it was successful (**Figure 1.45**) or if a problem occurred (**Figure 1.46**).

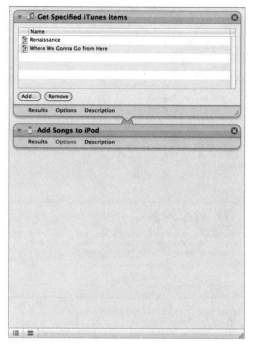

Figure 1.43 Actions, which have been inserted into Automator's workflow area.

Figure 1.44 Status of a running workflow.

Figure 1.45 Status of a successfully completed workflow.

Figure 1.46 Status of a problematic workflow.

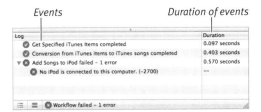

Events   *Duration of events*

Figure 1.47 Automator's log area.

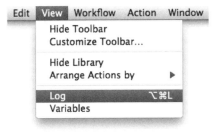

Figure 1.48 Choose Log from the View menu to display Automator's log area.

View Log button

Figure 1.49 Automator's log area at the bottom of a workflow window.

Viewing the workflow log area

The status area in Automator is great for quick updates. If you want a more detailed account of your workflow's status, however, you can consult Automator's log area. The log, which resides at the bottom of the workflow area, indicates which actions ran, whether they ran successfully, whether any conversion actions ran, and more. It also provides detailed information about any errors that may have occurred (**Figure 1.47**).

To view the workflow log area:

Choose View > Log (**Figure 1.48**).

or

Click the View Log button ▤ at the bottom of the workflow area (**Figure 1.49**).

or

Press Option ⌘ L.

The workflow log is displayed at the bottom of the workflow area.

✔ Tip

■ The workflow log can be a very valuable troubleshooting tool. Be sure to check it often!

Viewing the workflow variables area

If your workflow uses variables, the bottom of your workflow area can display a list of those variables as well. Here, you can configure your variables or drag them into various places within the workflow (**Figure 1.50**).

To view the workflow variables area:

Choose View > Variables (**Figure 1.51**).

or

Click the View WorkflowVariables button at the bottom of the workflow area (**Figure 1.52**).

A workflow variables list is displayed at the bottom of the workflow area.

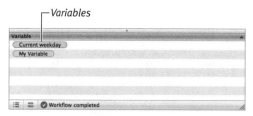

Figure 1.50 Automator's workflow variables area.

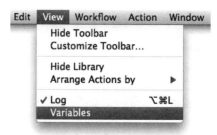

Figure 1.51 Choose Variables from the View menu to display Automator's workflow variables area.

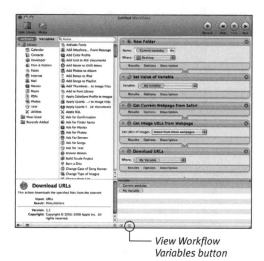

View Workflow Variables button

Figure 1.52 Automator's workflow variables area at the bottom of a workflow window.

GETTING TO KNOW AUTOMATOR'S INTERFACE

BUILDING SIMPLE WORKFLOWS

The best way to learn to use Automator is to dive in and build a practical workflow that accomplishes something you do repeatedly. Not only will such a project familiarize you with Automator's interface, it will show you how much of a difference the application can make in your unique workflow.

To help you get started, this chapter walks you through creating several simple workflows:

◆ **Email Daily Birthday Greetings.** Creates birthday greeting emails for anyone in your Address Book whose birthday is the current day.

◆ **Add Spotlight Comments to Photos.** Adds Spotlight comments to your digital photos, making them easier to search.

◆ **Email Photo Thumbnails.** Creates thumbnail versions of iPhoto images and inserts them into a new email message.

For each of these workflows, step-by-step instructions demonstrate how to create a workflow, locate the necessary actions, configure them, assemble them to form a completed workflow, and then save the workflow so you can use it outside of Automator. This chapter provides quick introductions to many of the topics discussed in detail later.

Email Daily Birthday Greetings

If you're like me, you're probably guilty of frequently forgetting people's birthdays. Have no fear, Automator can help! With only two actions, you can create a simple workflow that sends birthday greetings automatically.

Actions used:

◆ Find Address Book Items

◆ Send Birthday Greetings

To build the workflow:

1. Choose File > New (**Figure 2.1**).

   or

   Press ⌃ ⌘ N.

   A new workflow window and template selection panel appear (**Figure 2.2**).

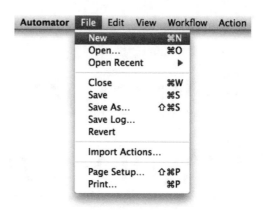

Figure 2.1 Creating a new workflow.

Figure 2.2 A new workflow window with the template selection panel.

iCal Alarm button   *Choose button*

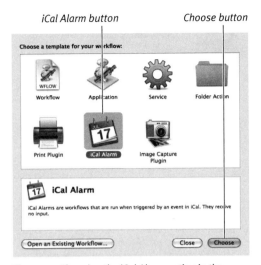

Figure 2.3 Choosing the iCal Alarm option in the template selection panel to create a scheduled workflow.

Empty workflow area

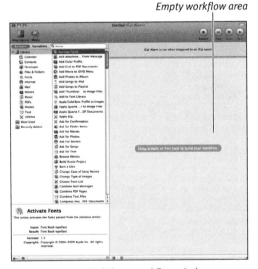

Figure 2.4 A new iCal Alarm workflow window, as created by Automator.

2. To create a scheduled workflow, click the iCal Alarm button in the template selection panel (**Figure 2.3**).

3. Click the Choose button in the template selection panel to create an empty workflow window. A header bar above the workflow areas indicates that the workflow will be run by an iCal event (**Figure 2.4**).

Now you're ready to begin adding actions to the workflow.

✔ Tips

■ If you notice an action in a screen shot in this book but don't see it on your own machine, don't worry. My machine has more than the default set of applications and actions installed.

■ The example workflows in this chapter feature actions arranged by category. If your actions are arranged by application, choose View > Arrange Applications by > Category (**Figure 2.5**) to match the examples.

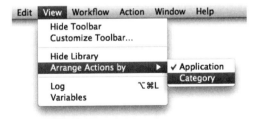

Figure 2.5 Setting Automator to arrange actions by category.

EMAIL DAILY BIRTHDAY GREETINGS

31

To add the Find Address Book Items action:

1. Click the Contacts category in the left column of the Library list (**Figure 2.6**).

   Automator lists that category's actions in the right column.

2. Click the Find Address Book Items action in the right column of the Library list (**Figure 2.7**).

3. Drag the Find Address Book Items action from the Library list into the workflow area (**Figure 2.8**).

   Automator displays an interface for the action within the workflow area (**Figures 2.9** and **2.10**).

Figure 2.6 Select the Contacts category in the Library list.

Figure 2.7 Select the Find Address Book Items action in the Library list.

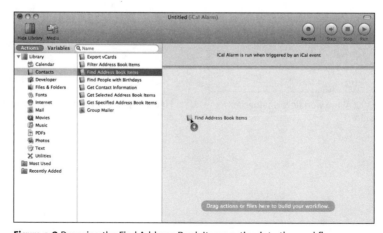

Figure 2.8 Dragging the Find Address Book Items action into the workflow area.

Figure 2.9 When added to the workflow area, the Find Address Book Items action's interface is displayed.

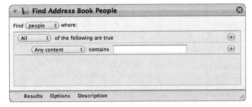

Figure 2.10 The Find Address Book Items action's interface.

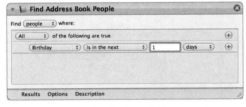

Figure 2.11 Configuring the Find Address Book Items action to locate people with a birthday in the next 24 hours.

4. Configure the settings on the action's interface to find people where **All** of the following are true – **Birthday** is in the next **1** days (**Figure 2.11**). This will limit the action's results to only people whose birthday falls within 1 day, or 24 hours, from the time the workflow runs.

✔ Tips

- Actions are listed in alphabetical order in the right column of the Library list.

- You can quickly navigate to an action by entering the first few characters of its name in the search field at the top of the Library list.

- In the workflow area, the Find Address Book Items action's title bar reflects how the action is configured. In this case, the action is set to find people, so the title of the action reads *Find Address Book People*.

- You might have noticed a Find People with Birthdays action in the Contacts category and wonder why it is not used here. At the time of this writing, a bug appeared in the Find People with Birthdays action, which caused the action to return no results. As a workaround, we're using the Find Address Book Items action. Once this bug is fixed, you can certainly use the Find People with Birthdays action instead.

- You may also be wondering why we didn't configure the Find Address Book Items action to find people whose birthday is *Today*. This is also due to an apparent bug, which caused the action to sometimes return no results.

EMAIL DAILY BIRTHDAY GREETINGS

To add the Send Birthday Greetings action:

1. Click the Mail category in the left column of the Library list (**Figure 2.12**).

   In the right column, Automator lists the actions in the Mail category.

2. Click to select the Send Birthday Greetings action in the right column of the Library list (**Figure 2.13**).

3. Drag the Send Birthday Greetings action from the Library list into the workflow area and drop it below Find Address Book Items.

   Automator displays an interface for the action within the workflow area (**Figures 2.14** and **2.15**).

Figure 2.12 Selecting the Mail category in the Library list.

Figure 2.13 Selecting the Send Birthday Greetings action in the Library list.

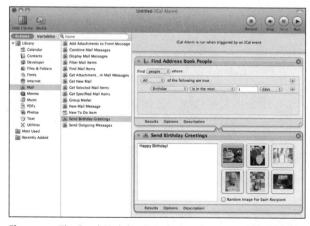

Figure 2.14 The Send Birthday Greetings action, once added into the workflow area.

EMAIL DAILY BIRTHDAY GREETINGS

Figure 2.15 The Send Birthday Greetings action's interface.

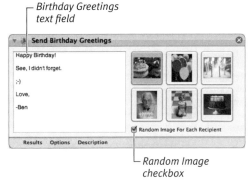

Figure 2.16 The Send Birthday Greetings action's interface with its settings configured.

Figure 2.17 The completed Email Daily Birthday Greetings workflow.

4. Type a birthday greeting into the text field in the action's interface (**Figure 2.16**).

5. Click the Random Image For Each Recipient checkbox in the action's interface (Figure 2.16).

It's that simple! The workflow is complete and ready to be tested and saved (**Figure 2.17**).

✔ Tips

- If you accidentally drop the Send Birthday Greetings action into the workflow window before Find Address Book Items, simply select the action's interface in the workflow area and drag it below the Find Address Book Items action's interface.

- Because this workflow uses Mail to send the birthday greetings, you must have an account configured in Mail to run this workflow.

- Because this workflow searches the Birthday field in Address Book, you must have dates entered there for the workflow to run successfully (**Figure 2.18**).

Figure 2.18 An Address Book entry with a birthday specified.

EMAIL DAILY BIRTHDAY GREETINGS

To test the workflow:

Click the Run button in Automator's toolbar at the top of the workflow (**Figure 2.19**).

Automator begins running the actions in your workflow. You can monitor its progress in the status area, located at the bottom of the workflow area (**Figure 2.20**).

As the workflow runs, it:

1. Opens Address Book.

2. Searches for and identifies people with a birthday in the next 24 hours.

3. Creates a new birthday greeting email in Mail for people found to have a birthday.

4. Personalizes each email with the first name of the person receiving the greeting (assuming it is entered in Address Book) and inserts your username into the subject of the email (**Figure 2.21**).

✔ Tip

■ To prevent unwanted emails from being sent while learning how to use Automator, this example workflow doesn't actually send the emails it generates. Rather, it leaves them opened in Mail, allowing you to look them over and then send them at your leisure, if desired. If you do want the workflow to send the messages, you can add the Send Outgoing Messages action, which is found in the Mail category of actions, to the end of your workflow (**Figure 2.22**).

Run button

Figure 2.19 The Run button in Automator's toolbar.

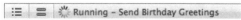

Figure 2.20 The status of the workflow as it runs.

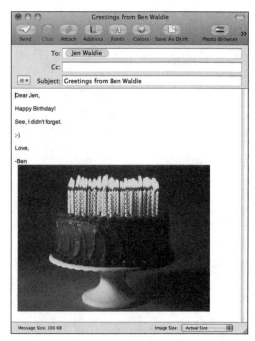

Figure 2.21 A birthday greeting email generated by the Email Daily Birthday Greetings workflow.

Figure 2.22 You can use the Send Outgoing Messages action to actually send the greetings.

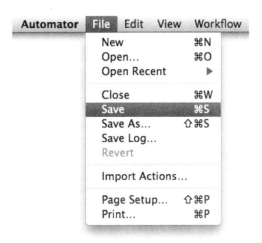

Figure 2.23 Saving the workflow.

Figure 2.24 Saving the workflow as an iCal Alarm.

Figure 2.25 Saving an iCal Alarm workflow produces a new event in iCal.

To save and schedule the workflow:

1. Choose File > Save (**Figure 2.23**).

   or

   Press ⌃⌘S.

   A Save iCal Alarm panel appears (**Figure 2.24**).

2. Enter Send Birthday Greetings into the Save iCal Alarm as field, and click Save.

   iCal is launched, and a new event is created with an Open File alarm set to open the workflow (**Figure 2.25**).

3. Set the event to an all-day event that repeats every day. Then set the event's alarm to run the day before, at 11:59 pm (**Figure 2.26**).

That's it! Now, every night at 11:59 PM, the workflow will run, find people in Address Book with a birthday in the next 24 hours, and create a birthday greeting email for them. When you wake up in the morning, all you need to remember is to click the Send button!

✔ Tip

■ Notice that iCal Alarm workflows are added to a calendar named Automator. This allows you to easily hide them from view, if desired. It also offers a quick way to delete all scheduled workflows simply by deleting the Automator calendar should the need ever arise.

Figure 2.26 You can set iCal to run the event on a schedule, such as every night at 11:59 PM.

EMAIL DAILY BIRTHDAY GREETINGS

Add Spotlight Comments to Photos

In Mac OS X, Spotlight makes searching for files a breeze—as long as they contain searchable text or descriptive names. If they don't, locating them can be a bit more difficult. Take digital photos, for example. Digital cameras typically assign nondescript unique numeric names, such as IMG_1234.JPG, to your photos. How can you quickly locate specific photos from a list of names like that?

Automator makes it easy. Adding meaningful comments to these files can help you find them later, and with Automator, you can create a workflow that assigns Spotlight comments to your photos.

Actions used:

◆ Ask for Finder Items

◆ Get Folder Contents

◆ Set Spotlight Comments for Finder Items

✔ Tip

■ Automator also includes a useful Spotlight action, which performs Spotlight searches and passes items it finds to later actions in a workflow for further processing.

Application button   Choose button

Figure 2.27 Creating a workflow Application using the template selection panel.

To build the workflow:

1. Choose File > New.

or

Press ⌃ ⌘ N.

A new workflow window and template selection panel appear.

2. Click the Application button in the template selection panel to create a workflow application (**Figure 2.27**).

3. Click the Choose button in the template selection panel.

Automator creates a workflow window with a header bar at the top of the workflow area. This header indicates that the workflow will receive files and folders as input (**Figure 2.28**).

✔ Tip

■ Although a workflow Application does not, some types of workflows display configuration options in the header bar above the workflow area, allowing you to control how the workflow will behave when run.

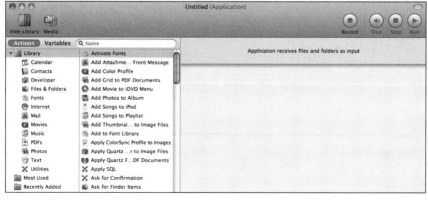

Figure 2.28 A workflow Application contains a header bar showing that it receives files and folders as input.

To add the Get Folder Contents action:

1. Click the Files & Folders category in the left column of the Library list (**Figure 2.29**) to see the related list of actions in the right column.

2. Select the Get Folder Contents action in the right column of the Library list (**Figure 2.30**), and drag it into the work-flow area (**Figure 2.31**).

3. Click the "Repeat for each subfolder found" checkbox on the action's interface (**Figure 2.32**).

   With this option selected, when you choose a folder containing other folders, the workflow processes the contents of those subfolders as well.

✔ Tip

■ Why do you need to get the contents of the specified folder? If you don't first get the folder's contents, the next action adds Spotlight comments to just the folder itself.

Figure 2.29 Selecting the Files & Folders category in the Library list.

Figure 2.30 Selecting the Get Folder Contents action in the Library list.

Figure 2.31 The Get Folder Contents action, once added into the workflow area.

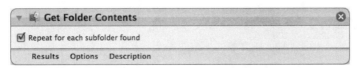

Figure 2.32 The Get Folder Contents action's interface, once its settings have been configured.

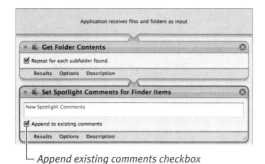

— Append existing comments checkbox

Figure 2.33 The Set Spotlight Comments for Finder Items action, once added into the workflow area.

— Show when run checkbox

— Options button

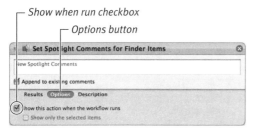

Figure 2.34 Configuring the Set Spotlight Comments for Finder Items action to "Show this action when the workflow runs."

To add the Set Spotlight Comments for Finder Items action:

1. Drag the Set Spotlight Comments for Finder Items action from the right column of the Library list (in the Files & Folders category, which should still be selected) into the workflow area (**Figure 2.33**).

2. Verify that the "Append to existing comments" checkbox is selected in the action (Figure 2.33). If it is not, existing Spotlight comments will be overwritten!

3. Click the Options button at the bottom of the action.

   The action expands to display additional options (**Figure 2.34**).

4. Click the "Show this action when the workflow runs" checkbox at the bottom of the action (Figure 2.34) to instruct the action to prompt you to enter the desired Spotlight comments when the workflow is run.

The main part of the workflow is now complete and ready to be tested.

✔ Tip

■ If you'd rather replace existing Spotlight comments, deselect the "Append to existing comments" checkbox.

Before testing the workflow:

Recall that you chose to create a workflow Application, which accepts files and folders as input when run outside of Automator. To test this workflow in Automator, you must give it something to process, so you'll insert an Ask for Finder Items action at the beginning of the workflow.

1. From the Files & Folders category in the Library list, drag the Ask for Finder Items action to the beginning of the workflow, right before the Get Folder Contents action (**Figure 2.35**).

2. Enter Choose a folder of images to apply Spotlight comments to: into the Prompt text field of the Ask for Finder Items action.

   The text you type here will appear in a dialog when the workflow is run.

3. Verify that the Desktop option is specified in the "Start at" pop-up menu within the action's interface.

4. Select the Folders option from the Type pop-up menu to ensure that you are prompted for folders only when the workflow is run.

5. Verify that the Allow Multiple Selection checkbox is not selected on the action's interface to ensure that you're only prompted to choose a single folder.

   The configured action should appear as in **Figure 2.36**.

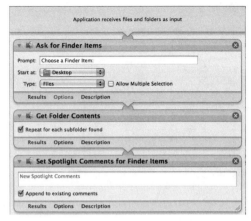

Figure 2.35 The Ask for Finder Items action as it appears when first added to a workflow.

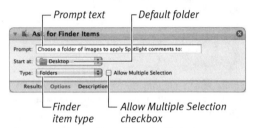

Figure 2.36 The configured Ask for Finder Items action.

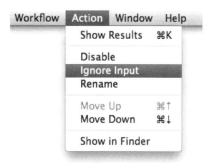

Figure 2.37 Setting the Ask for Finder Items action to ignore its input.

Figure 2.38 The completed Add Spotlight Comments to Photos workflow is ready for testing.

6. With the Ask for Finder Items action still selected in the workflow area, choose Action > Ignore Input (**Figure 2.37**).

Setting the action to ignore its input just tells Automator that the action doesn't need anything to be passed to it in order to run.

The test workflow is complete and ready to be run to make sure it works properly (**Figure 2.38**).

✔ Tip

- When configuring the Ask for Finder Items action, you can choose any folder that's convenient for you as the default.

To test the workflow:

1. Click the Run button in Automator's tool-bar at the top of the workflow.

   The Ask for Finder Items action runs first and prompts you to choose a folder of items.

2. Navigate to and select a folder of photos. For example, I chose a folder of images from an Arizona vacation (**Figure 2.39**).

   Ask for Finder Items then passes the chosen folder to the next action.

   The Get Folder Contents action retrieves a list of the items in the specified folder (received as input) and passes those items to the next action.

   The Set Spotlight Comments for Finder Items action runs next, and the action's window prompts you to enter some Spotlight comments.

3. Enter the desired comments. For example, I entered Grand Canyon and Sedona (**Figure 2.40**).

   The action now applies these comments to the items received from the previous action.

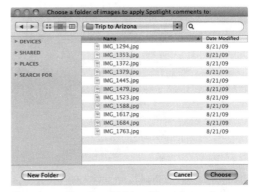

Figure 2.39 Choosing a folder of items to receive Spotlight comments.

Figure 2.40 Entering Spotlight comments to be applied to the items in the specified folder.

ADD SPOTLIGHT COMMENTS TO PHOTOS

Figure 2.41 Locating commented items using Spotlight.

Figure 2.42 Performing a Spotlight search from the menu bar.

To verify that the workflow was successful:

1. Press ⌃ ⌘ F in the Finder to perform a Spotlight search.

   A search window is displayed.

2. In the window's search field, enter the Spotlight comments that you typed when the workflow ran (**Figure 2.41**).

   Spotlight locates the items in the folder you chose while running the workflow (Figure 2.41).

✔ Tip

- You can also perform a Spotlight search from the search field in the upper-right corner of the Mac OS X menu bar (**Figure 2.42**).

ADD SPOTLIGHT COMMENTS TO PHOTOS

To save the workflow:

The workflow is now ready to be saved as an application. First, however, the Ask for Finder Items action must be disabled. Since the workflow Application will receive files and folders as input, this action is no longer necessary.

1. Select the Ask for Finder Items action in the workflow area, and choose Action > Disable (**Figure 2.43**).

   The Ask for Finder Items action should now appear compressed and grayed out in the workflow area (**Figure 2.44**).

2. Choose File > Save (**Figure 2.45**).

   A save panel appears.

3. Enter the name `Add Spotlight Comments to Photos`, verify that the File Format pop-up menu is set to Application, and choose the desired destination folder. Then click Save (**Figure 2.46**).

   The workflow is saved into the specified destination as an Application.

As the header bar above the workflow area indicated, workflow Applications receive files and folders as input. So, to process a folder of images, just drag it onto the saved application (**Figure 2.47**). With the exception of being prompted to choose a folder (which you disabled and is now being ignored), the workflow should proceed as it did when you ran your test within Automator.

Figure 2.47 Workflow Applications will process dropped files and folders as input.

Figure 2.43 Disabling the Ask for Finder Items action.

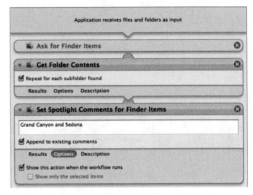

Figure 2.44 The completed workflow ready to be saved.

Figure 2.45 Saving the workflow.

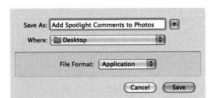

Figure 2.46 Specifying a name and location for the workflow Application.

Services button   *Choose button*

Figure 2.48 Creating a Service workflow using the template selection panel.

Figure 2.49 The header bar in a Services workflow.

Figure 2.50 Configuring the workflow to receive no input and to be available in Mail.

Figure 2.51 Manually locating the Mail application.

Email Photo Thumbnails

Want a quick way to email thumbnail versions of your latest and greatest digital photos to friends? Sure, you can do this from within iPhoto. But you can also do it with an Automator workflow without launching iPhoto.

Actions used:

◆ Ask for Photos

◆ Create Thumbnail Images

◆ Move Finder Items

◆ New Mail Message

To build the workflow:

1. Choose File > New.

   or

   Press ⌃⌘N.

   A new workflow window and template selection panel appear.

2. Click the Service button in the Starting Points panel (**Figure 2.48**).

3. Click the Choose button in the template selection panel.

   Automator opens a workflow window. In the header bar above the workflow area, some configuration options are displayed (**Figure 2.49**).

4. In the header bar above the workflow area, set the "Service receives" pop-up menu to "no input," and set the "in" pop-up menu to the Mail application. Verify that the "Replaces selected text" checkbox is not selected (**Figure 2.50**).

✔ Tip

■ If Mail doesn't appear in the "in" pop-up menu's list of applications, just choose Other, and you will be prompted to choose an application (**Figure 2.51**).

EMAIL PHOTO THUMBNAILS

47

To prepare the Ask for Photos action:

1. Click the Photos category in the left column of the Library list to display that category's actions in the right column (**Figure 2.52**).

2. Select the Ask for Photos action in the right column of the Library list, and drag it into the workflow area.

3. Type Choose some photos to email: in the Prompt text field of the Ask for Photos action (**Figure 2.53**).

   When the workflow is run, this text will be displayed at the top of the window that asks you to choose photos.

4. Verify that the "Allow multiple selection" checkbox is selected on the action's interface (Figure 2.53). Otherwise, you'd be able to select a single photo only!

✔ Tip

■ If you don't have iPhoto installed, you can still create this workflow. Just use an Ask for Files and Folders action in the Files & Folders category rather than an Ask for Photos action. As you follow along, just be aware that some of the steps will differ slightly.

Figure 2.52 Locating the Ask for Photos action and adding it to the workflow area.

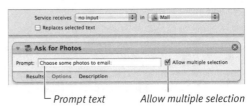

Prompt text   *Allow multiple selection*

Figure 2.53 The configured Ask for Photos action.

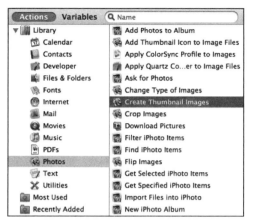

Figure 2.54 Locating the Create Thumbnail Images action.

To add the Create Thumbnail Images action:

The Photos category should still be selected in the Library list.

Select the Create Thumbnail Images action in the right column of the Library list, and drag it into the workflow area (**Figures 2.54** and **2.55**). You'll use the default settings for this action, so you don't need to change anything.

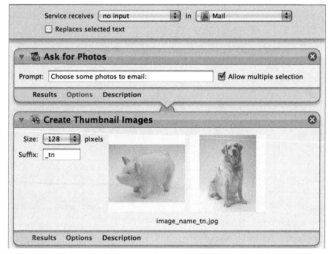

Figure 2.55 The Create Thumbnail Images action, once added to the workflow area.

To add the Move Finder Items action:

1. Click the Files & Folders category in the left column of the Library list to display its actions in the right column (**Figure 2.56**).

2. Drag the Move Finder Items action from the right column of the Library list into the workflow area.

The action is displayed within the workflow area (**Figure 2.57**) and by default is configured to move items to the desktop with the "Replacing existing files" checkbox deselected. No changes are necessary.

✔ Tip

■ The photos that you choose to process most likely reside within your iPhoto library folder, but you probably don't want to leave the thumbnails in your iPhoto library folder. The Move Finder Items action moves the thumbnails to your desktop.

Figure 2.56 The Files & Folders category of actions, displayed in the Library list.

Figure 2.57 The Move Finder Items action, once added into the workflow area.

Figure 2.58 Mail-related actions, displayed within the Library list.

To add the New Mail Message action:

1. Click the Mail category in the left column of the Library list to display that category's actions (**Figure 2.58**).

2. Click the New Mail Message action in the right column, and drag it into the workflow area.

    The action displays within the workflow area (**Figure 2.59**).

continues on next page

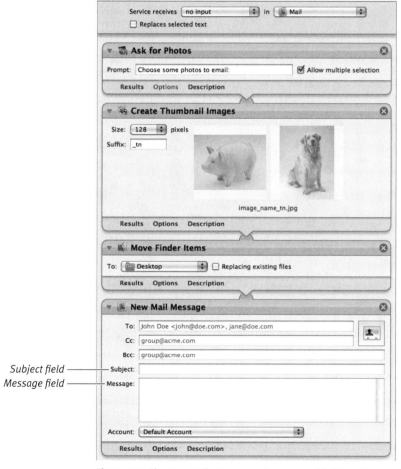

Subject field ———
Message field ———

Figure 2.59 The New Mail Message action, once added into the workflow area.

EMAIL PHOTO THUMBNAILS

3. Enter the desired text into the Subject and Message text fields in the action's interface (**Figure 2.60**).

The workflow is now complete and ready to be run (**Figure 2.61**).

✔ Tip

■ Because this workflow uses Mail to send the thumbnail images, you need an account configured in Mail to run the workflow.

Figure 2.60 The configured New Mail Message action.

Figure 2.61 The completed Email Photo Thumbnails workflow.

Figure 2.62 Choosing photos for processing by the workflow.

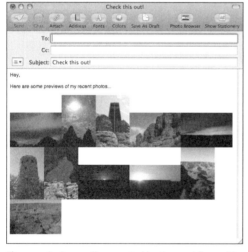

Figure 2.63 An email generated by the workflow with thumbnail images attached.

To test the workflow:

1. Click the Run button in Automator's toolbar at the top of the workflow.

   The workflow begins to run, and the Ask for Photos action prompts you to choose some photos from your iPhoto library.

2. Choose the desired photos (**Figure 2.62**).

3. The Create Thumbnail Images action runs next. It may take a few seconds because it generates thumbnail versions of the images that you chose.

4. The Move Finder Items action moves the thumbnail images to the desktop.

5. Finally, the workflow creates a new message in Mail that contains the subject and body that you specified in the New Mail Message action. Thumbnail versions of the specified images are attached (**Figure 2.63**).

✔ Tip

■ If you don't have iPhoto installed and your workflow contains an Ask for Finder Items action instead, you are prompted to locate image files on disk.

EMAIL PHOTO THUMBNAILS

To save the workflow:

The workflow is now ready to be saved as a Service.

1. Choose File > Save.

   A save panel appears.

2. Enter the name Email Photo Thumbnails. Then click Save (**Figure 2.64**).

   The workflow is saved as a Service.

To run the workflow, bring Mail to the front and choose Services > Email Photo Thumbnails from the Mail menu in the menu bar (**Figure 2.65**).

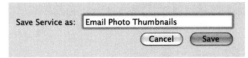

Figure 2.64 Saving the workflow as a Service.

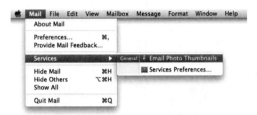

Figure 2.65 Running the Email Photo Thumbnails workflow within Mail.

3

WORKFLOW BASICS

So far, you've created a few simple Automator workflows. You should now be somewhat familiar with Automator's interface and how to use it. There's still more to learn, however. In this chapter, you'll begin exploring workflows in a bit more detail.

When building a workflow, figuring out what you want to automate is the easy part. Figuring out how to create the workflow takes more effort. You'll learn how to plan a workflow's tasks and then how to locate actions that can perform those tasks. You'll also learn more about creating, running, saving, and opening workflows.

For this chapter's examples, I've used the Add Spotlight Comments to Photos workflow from Chapter 2, "Building Simple Workflows." To follow along, create this workflow. Or, if you're feeling brave, create a new workflow of your own and jump right in.

Planning a Workflow

Before creating a workflow, take time to plan what you want it to do. For simple workflows, thinking about the overall job you want to accomplish is often enough. For complex workflows, however, writing an outline may be more helpful. An outline guides you through a workflow's creation, helps to prevent you from leaving out any steps along the way, and ensures that all of your actions are in the proper order. It sometimes also points out potential problem areas and allows you to consider workarounds for these up front.

To outline a workflow:

1. Think about the entire job you want to perform.

2. Divide the job into individual tasks, and make a list of these tasks: create a folder, rename the folder, move the folder, and so on.

3. Translate each task to an Automator action. To make this step easy, try to narrow down the list of actions by entering keywords into the search field in Automator's Library list.

✔ Tips

- If you're unsure of the exact tasks within a complicated workflow, go through the process manually and list the steps as you perform them.

- Look for helper workflows online. You may not find one that does exactly what you're trying to do, but you may find similar workflows that can point you in the right direction.

- Be sure to also think about how you will want to run the completed workflow, because this will dictate the type of workflow you create. For example, if you want a workflow that runs on a schedule, you'll need to create an iCal Alarm workflow.

Search field

Figure 3.1 To quickly locate an action, enter keywords into Automator's search field. Typing `folder` helps find the Ask for Finder Items action.

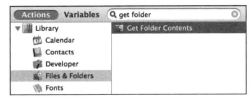

Figure 3.2 The keywords `get` and `folder` take you right to the Get Folder Contents action.

Figure 3.3 The `Spotlight` keyword displays a list of Spotlight-related actions.

Outlining an example workflow

Suppose you want to create a workflow that adds Spotlight comments to photos. An outline for this task might consist of three steps:

1. Locate a folder of photos.

2. Get a list of photos inside the folder.

3. Add Spotlight comments to the photos.

When you're ready to build the workflow, you must find Automator actions for the steps you've outlined.

Step 1: Locate the folder

1. Select the Files & Folders category in the Library list.

   Automator displays a list of actions related to files and folders.

2. Enter a keyword, such as `folder`, into the search field to narrow the list of actions.

3. Look for an action that does what you need. In this case, Ask for Finder Items should do the trick (**Figure 3.1**).

Step 2: Get the photos

Type the keywords `get folder` into the search field.

The Get Folder Contents action appears, which looks like it's just what you need (**Figure 3.2**).

Step 3: Add Spotlight comments

Enter `Spotlight` as a keyword; the Set Spotlight Comments for Finder Items action appears (**Figure 3.3**).

PLANNING A WORKFLOW

✔ Tips

■ Locating actions to do what you want may sound simple, but it's often easier said than done. It becomes easier with practice.

■ Not sure what an action does just by looking at its name? Check its description for more clues (**Figure 3.4**).

■ Using the search field in the Library list doesn't just search action names. It also searches keywords within actions, making it easier to find actions if you don't know their names (**Figure 3.5**).

■ If you can't find an action within Automator that performs a specific task, check the Automator section of Apple's Mac OS X Downloads page at www.apple.com/downloads/macosx/automator/ for third-party actions.

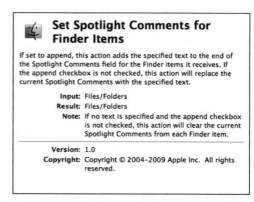

Figure 3.4 An action's description provides additional details about its function.

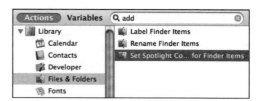

Figure 3.5 Searching for keywords can help you find an action when you're unsure of its name. Here, typing the keyword *add* helps find the Set Spotlight Comments for Finder Items action.

Automator Workflow Creation in a Nutshell

Think of creating Automator workflows as a four-step process:

◆ **Step 1.** Plan the workflow. Figure out what you want the workflow to do and how you want to run it.

◆ **Step 2.** Create the workflow. Add the actions and configure the settings and options.

◆ **Step 3.** Test the workflow in Automator, troubleshoot, and fix any problems. Make sure the steps are running smoothly.

◆ **Step 4.** Save the workflow so you can run it outside of Automator.

Be sure to check out Appendix A, "Workflow Creation Step-by-Step Guide," for a down-and-dirty guide to building workflows.

PLANNING A WORKFLOW

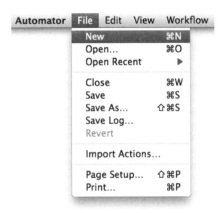

Figure 3.6 Creating a new Automator workflow.

Figure 3.7 The template selection panel allows you to choose the type of workflow you want to create.

Creating a Workflow

When you launch Automator, a new workflow window opens automatically. You can also create a new workflow at any time after Automator has been launched.

To create a workflow:

1. Choose File > New (**Figure 3.6**).

   or

   Press ⌃ ⌘ N.

   Anytime a new workflow window appears, a template selection panel displays (**Figure 3.7**). This panel allows you to choose the type of workflow you want to build. From this panel, you can create a Workflow file, an Application, a Service, a Folder Action, a Print Plugin, an iCal Alarm, or an Image Capture Plugin. The type you choose depends on how you want to use the workflow when it's finished. For example, if you want to run the workflow when you're in a specific application, such as Mail, you may want to create a Service. If you want to run the workflow whenever you download your digital photos, you may want to create an Image Capture Plugin. If you're unsure of how you want to run the workflow, just choose to create a Workflow, and you can convert it to a different type later.

continues on next page

2. Choose the desired type of workflow in the template selection panel, and then click Choose. For example, in Chapter 2, you chose Application for the Add Spotlight Comments to Photos workflow.

The panel disappears, and you're left with an empty workflow window. Depending on the type of workflow you chose to create, you may see some configuration options at the top of the workflow area (**Figure 3.8**).

You'll learn all about the different types of workflows, their configuration options, and how to save them in Chapter 5, "Types of Workflows." This chapter focuses mainly on Workflow files and Applications.

✔ Tips

■ You can open a saved Automator workflow from the template selection panel. To do so, click the Open an Existing Workflow button.

■ Clicking the Close button closes the template selection panel and the workflow window.

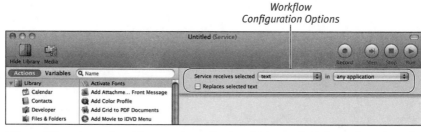

Figure 3.8 Some types of workflows, such as a Service, display configuration options above the workflow area.

CREATING A WORKFLOW

Figure 3.9 Choosing Run from the Workflow menu to run the current workflow.

Figure 3.10 Running a workflow by clicking the Run button in the Automator workflow window toolbar.

Running a Workflow within Automator

After you've finished creating a workflow, it's always a good idea to run it within Automator. Testing this way gives you quick access to valuable troubleshooting tools, such as Automator's log, and allows you to adjust the workflow by changing an action's settings, inserting a new action, or whatever else might be necessary. When it's running properly, you'll then want to save the workflow for use outside of Automator.

✔ Tips

- Although the process of running all types of workflows within Automator is pretty much the same, each type of workflow behaves differently once saved. Chapter 5 explains how different types of workflows are run outside of Automator.

- For advice on troubleshooting workflows, see Chapter 9, "Troubleshooting."

To run a workflow in Automator:

◆ Choose Workflow > Run (**Figure 3.9**).

or

Click the Run button in the workflow window toolbar (**Figure 3.10**).

or

Press ⌃ ⌘ R.

The workflow begins to run.

What you see as a workflow runs

As a workflow runs within Automator, you'll notice several things:

◆ The buttons in the workflow window's toolbar change. The Record button is disabled, the Stop button is enabled, and the Run button changes to Pause (**Figure 3.11**).

◆ The currently running action displays a progress spinner in its lower-left corner (**Figure 3.12**).

◆ If an action produces an error, Automator displays a red X in the lower-left corner of the action (**Figure 3.13**). The workflow then stops running.

Figure 3.11 The workflow window toolbar buttons change while a workflow is running.

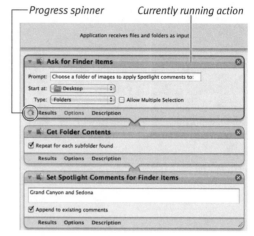

Figure 3.12 As a workflow runs within Automator, a spinner displays in the lower-left corner of the currently running action.

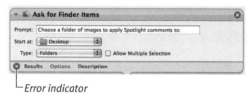

Figure 3.13 If an action generates an error while a workflow runs, a red X appears in the lower-left corner of that action.

Success indicator

Figure 3.14 A green checkmark displays in the lower-left corner of an action that runs successfully.

◆ After an action runs successfully, Automator displays a green checkmark in its lower-left corner (**Figure 3.14**) and proceeds to run the next action in the workflow.

◆ The bottom of the workflow window reports the overall status of your workflow, displaying the name of the currently running action, errors, or successful completion (**Figures 3.15**, **3.16**, and **3.17**).

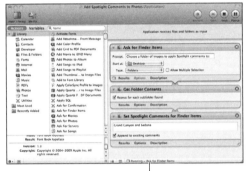

Currently running action

Figure 3.15 As a workflow runs, the bottom of the workflow window lists the currently running action.

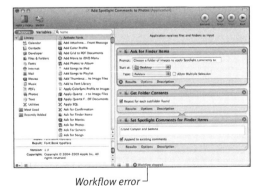

Workflow error

Figure 3.16 The bottom of the workflow window indicates when an error occurs.

Workflow successful

Figure 3.17 The bottom of the workflow window indicates when the workflow runs successfully.

RUNNING A WORKFLOW WITHIN AUTOMATOR

Saving a Workflow

After you've created and tested a workflow, you're ready to save it.

To save a workflow:

◆ If your workflow is a new workflow, choose File > Save (**Figure 3.18**) or press ⌃⌘S.

Or

◆ If your workflow is an existing workflow, choose File > Save or press ⌃⌘S to resave the workflow in its current location. If you don't want to overwrite your existing workflow, choose File > Save As (**Figure 3.19**) or press ⇧Shift⌃⌘S.

If you're not replacing an existing workflow, Automator displays a Save panel attached to the front workflow window. For Workflow files and Applications, this Save panel allows you to specify a name and destination folder for the workflow. You also have the option of changing the format of the workflow here, if you need to do so, to either a Workflow file or an Application (**Figures 3.20** and **3.21**).

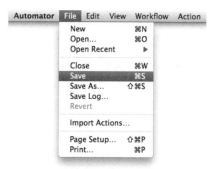

Figure 3.18 Save a new workflow by choosing File > Save.

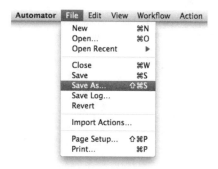

Figure 3.19 Save an existing workflow with a new name by choosing File > Save As.

Figure 3.20 When you save a Workflow file or Application, Automator displays a Save panel.

Figure 3.21 Automator allows you to toggle between Workflow files and Applications when saving.

SAVING A WORKFLOW

Figure 3.22 Automator only prompts you for a name when saving a Service, Folder Action, Print Plugin, iCal Alarm, and Image Capture Plugin workflow.

For Service, Folder Action, Print Plugin, iCal Alarm, and Image Capture Plugin workflows, a Save panel is also displayed, but it only allows you to specify a name for the workflow. You don't need to choose a destination folder. Rather, Automator handles saving it to the correct location for you automatically, based on the workflow type (**Figure 3.22**).

✔ Tips

- Chapter 5 discusses saving Service, Folder Action, Print Plugin, iCal Alarm, and Image Capture Plugin workflows in more detail, and explains where these workflows are stored once they're saved.

- When specifying a destination folder in a Save window, press ⌃ ⌘ D to quickly choose the Desktop as the desired location. Press Shift ⌃ ⌘ H to choose your Home folder.

SAVING A WORKFLOW

Opening a Workflow

Any workflow, regardless of its type, can be reopened in Automator for further editing.

To open a workflow:

1. Choose File > Open (**Figure 3.23**).

   or

   Press ⌃ ⌘ O.

   or

   Click the Open an Existing Workflow button in the template selection panel (**Figure 3.24**).

   The Open dialog appears.

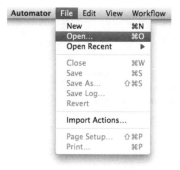

Figure 3.23 Open a workflow by choosing File > Open.

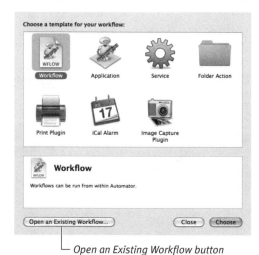

Open an Existing Workflow button

Figure 3.24 Workflows can also be opened from the template selection window.

Figure 3.25 The Open dialog allows you to choose the type of workflow you want to open.

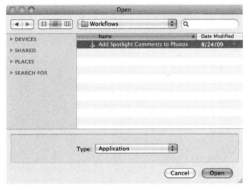

Figure 3.26 When the Open dialog appears, locate the workflow file you want to open, and click Open.

Figure 3.27 Previously opened workflows can be reopened by choosing File > Open Recent.

2. In the Open dialog, set the Type pop-up menu to the type of workflow you want to open.

Automator allows you to choose a workflow of the specified type. If you're unsure of the workflow's type, set the pop-up menu to display All workflows (**Figure 3.25**).

3. Locate the workflow and click Open (**Figure 3.26**).

The workflow opens in Automator. You can now modify the workflow, if desired, by inserting new actions, removing actions, or modifying action settings. When you're done, don't forget to test and resave the workflow.

✔ Tips

■ You can open recently opened workflows by choosing File > Open Recent (**Figure 3.27**).

■ You can quickly open any workflow by dragging it onto the Automator icon in your Dock. You can also open a Workflow file (not a workflow Application) by double-clicking it.

■ If you've received a workflow from a friend or have downloaded one from the web, it's good practice to open it in Automator before running it. Doing so allows you to preview what the workflow will do. It also lets you ensure that all the actions used by the workflow are installed on your machine, because Automator will alert you if they are not.

OPENING A WORKFLOW

Working with Actions

4

By now you should be comfortable creating basic workflows and getting around the main portions of Automator's interface. There's still a lot more of Automator to learn, though. To do anything truly useful, you need to add actions to your workflow, and you need to configure those actions to do what you want. This chapter helps you get to this next level by showing you how to:

◆ Find an action that's right for your workflow

◆ Add actions to your workflow and understand warning messages that may be displayed

◆ Configure an action's settings and options so the action will do what you want

◆ Adjust your workflow by renaming, deleting, and disabling actions

◆ Use action input and output values properly so that your actions work together when you run the workflow

The techniques you learn in this chapter will apply to working with virtually any action within an Automator workflow.

Locating Actions to Do What You Want

Automator comes with hundreds of actions, and that list grows every time you add new Automator-ready applications or third-party actions to your machine. With so many actions, locating the one to do what you want is no small feat. However, there are some practical ways to find them.

Picking the right action for a task

In Chapter 3, "Workflow Basics" (see "Planning a Workflow"), you learned that it's a good idea to think through the job of a workflow before creating it. Break it down into individual tasks, and then translate those tasks to actions.

But how do you pick the right action for a task? Think about the task. What does it do? For example, does it create a folder on the desktop? What is its result? The newly created folder? What application or process does it target? The Finder? Use the words from these questions and answers as keywords, and type them into Automator's search field to help find an appropriate action.

✔ Tip

■ Be sure to check action descriptions frequently, because they often contain important information. See "Viewing an Action's Description" later in this chapter.

Five Useful File & Folder Actions

1. **Find Finder Items.** Helps you locate specific files and folders on your Mac when your workflow runs.

2. **Filter Finder Items.** Allows you to filter a list of files for ones matching specific criteria. For example, you could use this action to filter for only image files.

3. **Sort Finder Items.** Use this action to sort Finder items into the order you want to process them. This can be especially useful if you want to process files sequentially or in the order they were last modified.

4. **Connect to Servers.** Does your workflow process files and folders on a server volume? Use this action to make sure that server volume is connected when your workflow runs.

5. **Set Spotlight Comments for Finder Items.** Spotlight searching makes locating files a breeze. Use this action to ensure that files without descriptive names, such as your digital photos, are found when you perform a search.

Library ⌐

Clear search field button ⌐

Search field ⌐

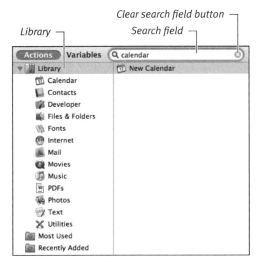

Figure 4.1 Searching for calendar actions using a keyword.

To locate an action by application name, action name, or keyword:

1. In your workflow window, click Library in the left column of the Library list to display a list of all available actions (**Figure 4.1**).

2. In the search field at the top of the Library list, type a search term, such as an application name, action name, or a keyword. For example, to find an action that creates a new calendar in iCal, you might enter `iCal` or `calendar`.

    Automator lists any actions that match the specified criteria (Figure 4.1).

3. Scan through the list of found actions and look for one that does what you need. Then drag it into your workflow.

✔ Tips

■ If you're having trouble locating an action using one keyword, try a synonym. For example, if you want to locate an action that will search for something, try the keywords `search` and `find`.

■ If no actions are found by your search, verify that you have clicked Library at the top of the left column in the Library list.

■ Click the X button on the right side of the search field to clear the search and display other actions again (Figure 4.1).

■ If you've tried and tried, but are unable to locate an action, see if a third-party developer has created one. Search Apple's Mac OS X Automator action download site at www.apple.com/downloads/macosx/automator/.

To locate all actions within a category:

1. Ensure that Automator's Library list is arranged by category. If it's not, choose View > Arrange Actions by > Category (**Figure 4.2**).

2. Click the desired category name within the Library list.

   Automator displays the actions within that specific category (**Figure 4.3**).

   Now you can scan through the list of actions within the category for the desired action or actions. When you find what you're looking for, drag it into your workflow.

✔ Tip

- If actions don't fit into a specific category, they'll be in the category Other. Check in that category if you can't find the action you want. If you don't see the Other category, all of your actions fit into Automator's built-in categories.

To locate all actions for a given application:

1. You may find it easier to locate actions by application rather than by category. To do this, first ensure that the Library list is arranged by application. If it's not, choose View > Arrange Actions by > Application (**Figure 4.4**).

2. Click the appropriate application name within the Library list to display the actions that pertain to that specific application (**Figure 4.5**). For example, to see all iCal-related actions, click iCal.

3. Scan through the list of application actions for one that does what you need, and then insert it into your workflow.

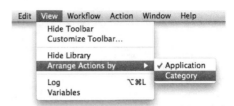

Figure 4.2 Configuring Automator's Library list to arrange actions by category.

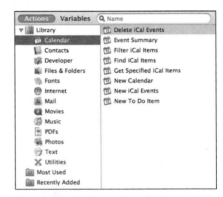

Figure 4.3 Selecting a category of actions.

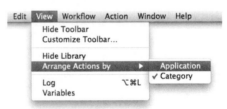

Figure 4.4 Configuring Automator's Library list to arrange actions by application.

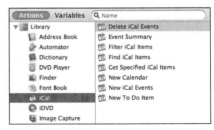

Figure 4.5 Selecting an application to display all actions for that application.

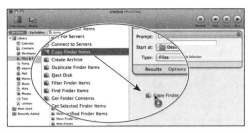

Figure 4.6 Dragging an action into a workflow.

Figure 4.7 An action's interface, once added to a workflow.

Inserting Actions into a Workflow

You already know that you can add an action to your workflow by selecting it in the Library list and dragging it to the desired spot in your workflow. You can also insert an action at the end of your workflow by double-clicking it in the Library list (**Figures 4.6** and **4.7**).

✔ Tip

■ If you've accidentally added an action to the wrong place in a workflow, simply select it and drag it to the correct location.

Four Useful Actions for Advanced Automator Users

1. **Run AppleScript.** Automator's a great tool, but as discussed in the Introduction, it has some limitations that can be overcome with AppleScript functions. This action allows you to paste in AppleScript code, so that it runs as part of your workflow.

2. **Run Shell Script.** This action provides even greater possibilities for creating robust workflows by providing access to the UNIX underpinnings of Mac OS X. Just paste in the desired shell commands to incorporate them into your workflow.

3. **Loop.** Need to create a workflow that runs over and over again? As you'll learn in Chapter 7, "Workflow Looping," this action allows you to do just that.

4. **Set/Get Value of Variable.** Does your workflow include actions in different locations that need to share information? As you'll learn in Chapter 8, "Using Variables," this pair of actions allows you to store the output of an action in memory and then refer back to it later in your workflow.

Understanding action insertion warnings

Sometimes when you drag an action into a workflow, Automator displays an alert panel. This generally occurs when the action you're adding will modify files, folders, or other data in some irreversible way. The type of warning displayed determines how you handle it.

◆ Some warnings simply alert you to something important. In these cases, you can usually choose to continue adding the action to the workflow, or you can decide not to add the action and simply cancel the alert (**Figure 4.8**).

◆ Other warnings provide a message and suggest adding another action first, usually to avoid potential data loss. In these cases, you can choose to cancel, add the suggested action in addition to the action you've dragged into the workflow, or insert only the action you've dragged into the workflow (**Figure 4.9**).

If you click Add, Automator inserts the suggested action immediately before the action you dragged into the workflow (**Figure 4.10**).

If you click Don't Add, Automator adds only the action you dragged into the workflow.

If you click Cancel, the workflow remains unchanged.

Figure 4.8 An insertion warning for the Delete iCal Events action. Clicking Continue adds the action to the workflow. Clicking Cancel leaves the workflow as it is.

Figure 4.9 An insertion warning displayed by the Scale Images action asks if you'd like to add a Copy Finder Items action to prevent data loss.

Figure 4.10 An auto-inserted Copy Finder Items action precedes the Scale Images action to prevent data loss.

Disable future alerts checkbox

Figure 4.11 Action alerts give you the option of disabling future alerts.

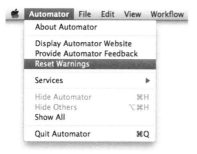

Figure 4.12 Enabling all action alerts.

✔ Tips

■ When it comes to potential data loss, it's better to be safe than sorry. Don't be afraid to add a suggested action to your workflow. You can always remove it if you decide later that you don't need it.

■ Tired of seeing action alerts? To insert an action into a workflow without displaying its action insertion warning, hold ⇧ (Shift) while dragging the action into the workflow area. This will not permanently disable the alert for that particular action.

■ You can also disable all action alerts by selecting the "Do not show this message again" checkbox in any alert window (**Figure 4.11**).

■ You can enable all disabled action alerts by choosing Automator > Reset Warnings from the menu bar (**Figure 4.12**).

Insertion Warnings and the Actions That Cause Them

Two common types of actions that cause insertion warnings include:

◆ **Deletion Actions.** Most actions that permanently delete something display a warning of some type when inserted into a workflow. For example, the Remove Empty Playlists action lets you know that once you run it, there's no way to get those playlists back (**Figure 4.13**).

◆ **File Manipulation Actions.** Most actions that modify files display a warning letting you know that those modifications can't be undone. If you want to retain your originals, consider adding an action, such as a Copy Finder Items or Create Archive action, to back up your files prior to modifying them (**Figure 4.14**).

Figure 4.13 An alert displayed by a deletion action.

Figure 4.14 An alert displayed by a file manipulation action.

Viewing an Action's Description

Each Automator action has a description that provides an overview of the action, the types of input the action accepts, the types of output the action produces, and more—a treasure trove of information for any Automator user. You can view an action's description in the Library list or in the workflow area.

To view the description of an action in the Library list:

◆ In the Library list, select the action you want to view to see its description in the workflow window's lower-left corner (**Figure 4.15**).

✔ Tips

■ If you're unsure of an action's function or one of its settings, check its description.

■ If the description area is not visible in the lower left of the workflow window, click the ▣ icon at the bottom of the window to display it.

To view the description of an action in the workflow area:

◆ Click the Description button at the bottom of the action's interface. The action's interface expands to show its description (**Figure 4.16**). To hide the description, click the Description button again.

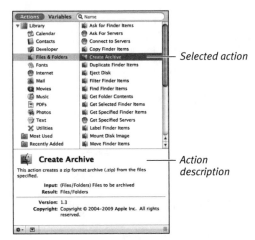

Selected action

Action description

Figure 4.15 Viewing the description of the Create Archive action in the Library list.

Description button — Action description

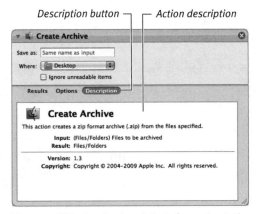

Figure 4.16 Viewing the description of an action in the workflow area.

Figure 4.17 The New iCal Events action has settings that can modify its behavior.

Modifiable settings

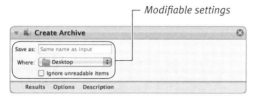

Figure 4.18 Modifiable settings for the Create Archive action.

Modifiable settings

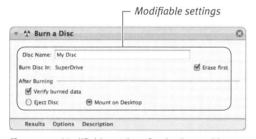

Figure 4.19 Modifiable settings for the Burn a Disc action.

Action Settings

Many actions have settings you can change to control the action's behavior when you run the workflow. Take the New iCal Events action, for example (**Figure 4.17**). This action allows you to specify a calendar and title for the event along with a start and end time, an alarm, and more. When run within a workflow, this action behaves according to the settings you've specified.

Whenever you add an action to a workflow, you should check to see whether the action contains any modifiable settings, and if so, adjust them accordingly.

Actions with settings

It's difficult to talk about individual action settings. Because every action performs a different task, each action's settings are different. When you begin working with a new action, you need to become familiar with its settings so you can make it do what you want.

To understand how modifying the settings on an action affects how it behaves when run, experiment with some examples:

◆ The Create Archive action's settings allow you to specify the name and location of the archive and whether any unreadable items should be ignored (**Figure 4.18**).

◆ The Burn a Disc action's settings enable you to specify the name of the disc, whether it should be erased first, whether it should be verified, and whether it should be ejected or mounted on the desktop after burning (**Figure 4.19**).

continues on next page

ACTION SETTINGS

◆ The New Mail Message action's settings allow you to specify the To, Cc, and Bcc recipients, the subject, the message content, and the account for the message (**Figure 4.20**).

✔ Tip

■ Don't be afraid to try new things. If you're unsure of what an action setting does, try running the action in a test workflow to find out. Just be careful. If the action deletes or changes something, make sure you test it with data you don't mind deleting or changing.

Actions without settings

Some actions don't have modifiable settings. The interface for such an action is simply a title bar and a footer area—rather plain, as you can see (**Figure 4.21**).

✔ Tip

■ Looking for an action setting that doesn't exist? Developers try to provide action settings that users will need to change on a regular basis. But they often don't think of everything. If you need a specific action setting that doesn't exist, let the action's developer know about it, and perhaps it will be added in a future release.

Modifiable settings

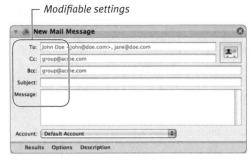

Figure 4.20 Modifiable settings for the New Mail Message action.

Figure 4.21 The Get Selected Finder Items action does not contain modifiable settings.

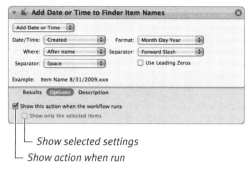

— Show selected settings

— Show action when run

Figure 4.22 Configuring the Rename Finder Items action to allow its settings to be adjusted when run within a workflow.

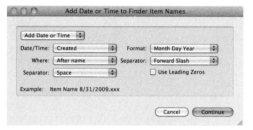

Figure 4.23 The Rename Finder Items action's interface, as displayed when run within a workflow, allows its settings to be adjusted.

Action Options

Configuring an action's settings in advance can be helpful, but for some situations you may need to change the action's settings when the workflow runs. For example, suppose you're creating a workflow that creates a new email message in Mail. Rather than using the same settings every time, you may want to change the subject, message content, and more each time the workflow runs.

Allowing an action's settings to be adjusted when the workflow runs is also extremely helpful in a workflow that you're giving to other people. Users can then modify the workflow's behavior to meet their unique needs.

Many Automator actions can be set to show their settings when run, and this can often make your workflow more flexible.

To configure an action to allow all its settings to be modified when run:

1. Click the Options button at the bottom of the action.

   The action's interface expands to display some additional configuration options.

2. Select the "Show this action when the workflow runs" checkbox (**Figure 4.22**).

Now when the workflow is run, the interface for the action is displayed, allowing the action's settings to be adjusted as needed (**Figure 4.23**).

Some actions allow you to be a bit more selective with regard to which of the action's settings may be modified. Rather than allowing all of the action's settings to be adjusted when the workflow is run, you can pick and choose the ones that you'd like to be modifiable.

continues on next page

✔ Tips

- If an action is configured to allow its settings to be modified when the workflow runs, any preconfigured settings serve as the default settings for the action.

- Even if you've configured an action with modifiable settings, it's still a good idea to enter some defaults. Enter the settings that you expect to be used most often when the action is run. This will save you time when the workflow runs, because you won't need to adjust settings unless changes are needed.

- If an action's Options button is disabled, the action cannot be configured to allow settings modification at runtime (**Figure 4.24**).

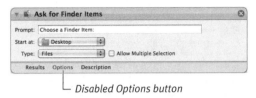

— *Disabled Options button*

Figure 4.24 The Ask for Finder Items action's settings cannot be adjusted when the workflow is run.

ACTION OPTIONS

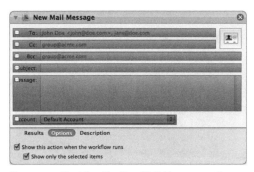

Figure 4.25 Enabling the New Mail Message action to show selected settings when run.

Selected settings

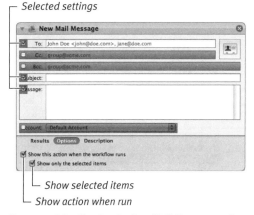

Show selected items

Show action when run

Figure 4.26 Configuring the New Mail Message action to allow only specified settings to be adjusted when run within a workflow.

Figure 4.27 Specified adjustable settings for the New Mail Message action's interface, as displayed when run within a workflow.

To configure an action to allow only specified settings to be modified when run:

1. Select the "Show this action when the workflow runs" checkbox in the Options area.

2. Select the "Show only the selected items" checkbox in the Options area.

   The settings within the action's interface become highlighted with checkboxes displayed next to them (**Figure 4.25**).

3. Select the checkboxes next to any settings that you'd like to be adjustable at runtime (**Figure 4.26**).

   Now when the workflow is run, only the settings you selected are displayed, allowing users to adjust only these as needed (**Figure 4.27**).

✔ Tip

■ If an action does not allow a subset of settings to be modified at runtime, the "Show only the selected items" checkbox in the Options area is disabled (Figure 4.22).

Deleting Actions

As you build a workflow, you may place the wrong action or change your mind about whether to include a certain action—hey, it happens. Don't worry; you can delete the undesirable action.

To delete an action from a workflow:

1. Select the action in the workflow area.

2. Press the Delete key.

   or

   Click the X button on the right side of the action's title bar (**Figure 4.28**).

   or

   Choose Edit > Delete (**Figure 4.29**).

   The action disappears from the workflow. If any actions were below it, they move up to fill in the gap.

✔ Tips

- A note of warning: When you delete an action from a workflow, you will not be prompted to confirm your intent. Rather, Automator deletes the action immediately, settings and all. So, before you choose to delete an action, make sure that you really want to delete it. If you're unsure, try disabling it instead (see the next section).

- If you do accidentally delete an action, you can try to get it back by pressing ⌘Z or by choosing Edit > Undo Remove Action (**Figure 4.30**).

Delete button

Figure 4.28 Deleting an action from a workflow.

Figure 4.29 Deleting the selected action in a workflow.

Figure 4.30 Sometimes, the deletion of an action can be undone.

Figure 4.31 Disabling the selected action in a workflow.

Figure 4.32 Disabling an action within a workflow from the action's contextual menu.

Figure 4.33 A disabled action.

Figure 4.34 Enabling the selected disabled action in a workflow.

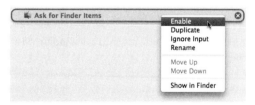

Figure 4.35 Enabling a disabled action within a workflow.

Disabling Actions

Instead of completely deleting an action from a workflow, you way want to disable it. This can be useful for testing purposes, because disabling the action allows you to see how your workflow behaves without the action. If the workflow works well, you can then delete the action. One extremely helpful benefit of disabling an action is that if you do change your mind, you can always enable the action and you won't lose any of the settings that you may have configured.

To disable an action in a workflow:

1. Select the action in the workflow area.

2. Choose Action > Disable (**Figure 4.31**).
   or
   While holding down the Control key, click the action's title bar to display the contextual menu and choose Disable (**Figure 4.32**).

After you disable an action, it appears dimmed within the workflow (**Figure 4.33**). When you run your workflow, the action is simply ignored.

To enable a disabled action:

1. Select the disabled action.

2. Choose Action > Enable (**Figure 4.34**).
   or
   While holding down the Control key, click the action's title bar to display the contextual menu and choose Enable (**Figure 4.35**).

The action regains its normal appearance and runs as part of your workflow again.

Moving Actions

As your workflow takes shape, you may have to move actions to new locations in the workflow. Automator makes this easy.

To move an action up or down in a workflow:

1. Select the action.

2. Press ⌃⌘↑ to move the selected action up one step, or press ⌃⌘↓ to move it down one step.

   or

   Choose Action > Move Up to move the selected action up one step or Action > Move Down to move down one (**Figure 4.36**).

   or

   While holding down the (Control) key, click the title bar of the action to display the contextual menu and choose Move Up to move the action up or Move Down to go the opposite way (**Figure 4.37**).

To move an action into a specific location within a workflow:

1. Select the action in the workflow area.

2. Click the action's title bar, and drag it to the desired location within the workflow (**Figure 4.38**).

✔ Tip

- Dragging an action to a new location is the fastest way to move an action to the right spot in a long workflow.

Figure 4.36 Moving the selected action down in a workflow.

Figure 4.37 Moving an action down in a workflow using the action's contextual menu.

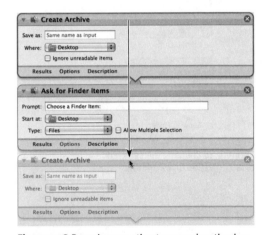

Figure 4.38 Dragging an action to a new location in a workflow.

Figure 4.39 Copying a selected action to the clipboard.

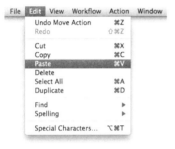

Figure 4.40 Pasting an action into the currently selected workflow.

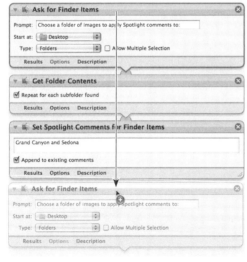

Figure 4.41 Copying an action from one location to another.

Copying Actions

Sometimes you want an action to stay put, but you need another copy of it elsewhere. You can do this by copying the action and then pasting it into the desired location in your workflow or even in a different workflow entirely.

Copying and relocating actions, method 1:

1. Select the action in the workflow area and choose Edit > Copy to copy the action to the clipboard (**Figure 4.39**).

   or

   Press ⌃ ⌘ C.

2. Select the workflow in which you want to insert the copied action. You can use the same workflow or a different one.

3. Choose Edit > Paste (**Figure 4.40**).

   or

   Press ⌃ ⌘ V.

   Automator pastes the action at the end of the workflow. If you pasted into the same workflow, the action now resides in two places.

Copying and relocating actions, method 2:

1. Select the action in the workflow area.

2. While holding down the Option key, drag the action to the desired location.

   Automator copies the action to that location (**Figure 4.41**).

continues on next page

COPYING ACTIONS

Copying and relocating actions, method 3:

1. Select the action in the workflow area.

2. Drag the action from the current work-flow into the desired location in a different workflow (**Figure 4.42**).

   Automator copies the action to the other workflow.

✔ Tip

■ When you copy an action, Automator retains the settings you configured for the original action in the pasted action.

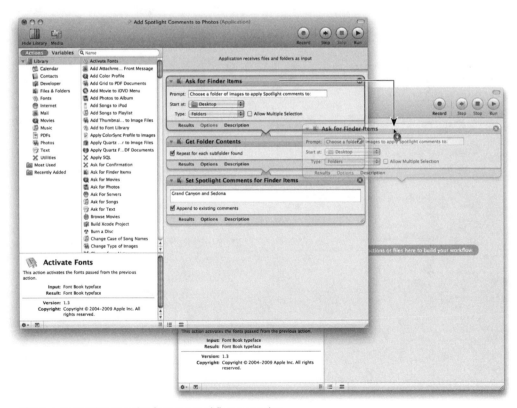

Figure 4.42 Copying an action from one workflow to another.

Figure 4.43 Renaming the selected action in a workflow.

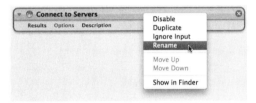

Figure 4.44 Renaming an action within a workflow from the action's contextual menu.

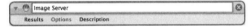

Figure 4.45 Renaming the Connect to Servers action.

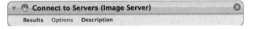

Figure 4.46 The Connect to Servers action is renamed to Ask for Images Folder.

Renaming Actions

While building a workflow, there may be times when you'd like an action's name to be a bit more descriptive than the default name. Take the Connect to Servers action, for example. Renaming this action to include the name of the server volume to which it connects would be helpful. You can rename a workflow's action in two steps.

To rename an action:

1. Select the action in the workflow area and choose Action > Rename (**Figure 4.43**).

   or

   While holding down the Control key, click the action's title bar to open the contextual menu and choose Rename (**Figure 4.44**).

   The action's name in the title bar becomes editable.

2. In the field, type the desired name and press the Return key (**Figure 4.45**).

   The action's title bar now displays the action's new name in parentheses after the original name for the action (**Figure 4.46**).

✔ Tips

- Renaming an action is a good way to insert a comment into a workflow. This is especially helpful if you're distributing your workflow to other people who may need to edit it.

- Renaming only affects an action within your workflow. Within the Library list, the action retains its original name.

Collapsing Actions

As you begin creating longer workflows, you may find that you're scrolling a lot to reach an action. There is a solution to this tedious task. Automator makes it easy to collapse individual actions, enabling you to view more of your workflow at a time, which means less scrolling. Collapsing an action condenses the action's interface down to a single title bar, hiding the action's settings, options, description, and so on.

To collapse an action in the workflow area:

◆ Double-click the action's title bar (**Figure 4.47**).

 or

 Click the small disclosure triangle to the left of the action's name in the title bar.

To expand a collapsed action in the workflow area:

◆ Double-click the title bar of the action (**Figure 4.48**).

 or

 Click the small disclosure triangle to the left of the action's name in the title bar again.

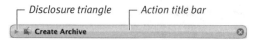

Figure 4.47 A collapsed action in the workflow area.

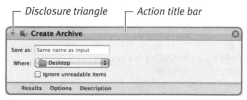

Figure 4.48 An expanded action in the workflow area.

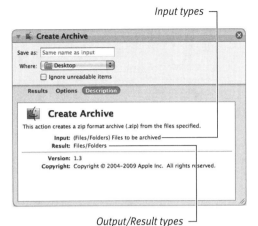

Input types

Output/Result types

Figure 4.49 Viewing the input and result types for the Create Archive action.

Working with Input and Output Values

Actions can talk to each other. As you learned in Chapter 1, "Getting Started," most actions can receive information (called *input*) from a previous action, and they can pass information (called *output*) to the next action in a workflow sequence. This process allows actions to work together like an assembly line, passing information along from one action to the next.

Matching action input and output values

Some actions can receive any kind of input and can live anywhere in a workflow. Many actions, however, need a specific kind of input to work properly. These actions must be placed into a workflow immediately following an action that provides the right kind of output. For example, an action that takes files and folders as input must come after an action that produces files and folders as output.

An action's description indicates the kind of input it needs as well as the kind of output (result) it generates (**Figure 4.49**).

continues on next page

Three Action Gems

Automator includes dozens of great actions that are sure to benefit the workflows of many. Here are a few very useful ones:

1. **Spotlight.** Need to find files to process when your workflow runs? Check out this action. It performs a Spotlight search for the specified criteria and passes the results down to the next action for further processing.

2. **Burn a Disc.** This great action burns files and folders directly to a CD or DVD. Consider using this action to create a workflow that backs up your modified files to DVD once per week.

3. **Text to Audio File.** This action can actually convert input text to audio format. In a hurry, and don't have time to read your email at your desk? Why not process it with this action, and listen to it on your iPod or iPhone?

When actions are placed together in a workflow, Automator checks if their input and output information matches. If it does, Automator links the actions visually (**Figure 4.50**). If the actions don't match, they appear separated (**Figure 4.51**). These visual clues can help you determine whether information will pass through your workflow as expected.

✔ Tip

- Mismatched actions don't always cause a problem. Whenever a mismatch occurs, Automator tries to convert the input and output values of the actions to matching types using a conversion action. For more on conversion actions, see the sidebar in the "About Actions" section in Chapter 1.

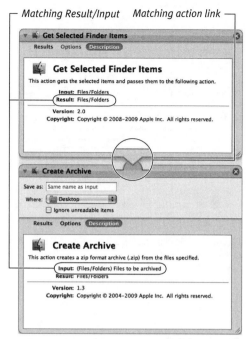

Figure 4.50 Two properly matched actions within a workflow, passing Files/Folders between one another.

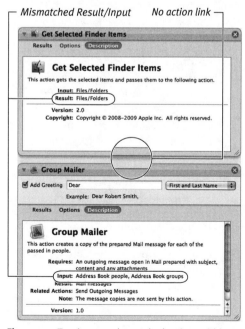

Figure 4.51 Two improperly matched actions within a workflow.

Downloaded files will be passed as input to the New Mail Message action

Figure 4.52 An example workflow, which downloads URLs from the current webpage in Safari and sends out an email notice when complete.

Ignoring an action's input

There may be times when you don't want an action to do anything with the input it receives. For example, **Figure 4.52** shows a workflow that retrieves URLs from a current webpage in Safari, downloads those URLs, and then sends out an email notice. This workflow consists of four actions:

◆ Get Current Webpage from Safari

◆ Get Link URLs from Webpages

◆ Download URLs

◆ New Mail Message

In this workflow, the Download URLs action passes downloaded files as input to the New Mail Message action. The New Mail Message action then adds those files as attachments to the Mail message that it creates. Although that's a nice feature, you may just want to send a notice that the files have been downloaded without actually attaching the downloaded files. To do this, you can tell the New Mail Message action to ignore its input.

continues on next page

To tell an action to ignore its input:

◆ In the workflow area, select the action whose input you'd like to ignore and choose Action > Ignore Input (**Figure 4.53**).

or

While holding down the [Control] key, click the action's title bar to display the contextual menu and choose Ignore Input (**Figure 4.54**).

The action becomes visually separated from the preceding action in the workflow, indicating that the action no longer accepts input (**Figure 4.55**).

After you disable an action's input, you can turn it back on again should the need arise.

✔ Tip

■ Not all actions can be told to ignore their input. If an action won't let you do this, the Ignore Input option is disabled in the Action menu, as well as in the action's contextual menu. Download URLs is one such action (**Figure 4.56**).

Figure 4.53 Telling the selected action in a workflow to ignore its input.

Figure 4.54 Telling the New Mail Message action to ignore its input from the action's contextual menu.

Figure 4.56 The Download URLs action won't allow its input to be ignored.

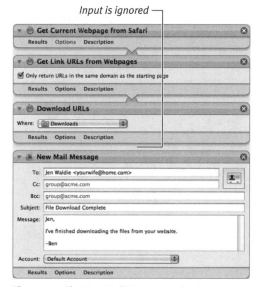

Input is ignored

Figure 4.55 The New Mail Message action is configured to ignore its input in a workflow.

Figure 4.57 Telling the selected action in a workflow to accept its input.

Figure 4.58 Telling the New Mail Message action to accept its input from the action's contextual menu.

Input is accepted

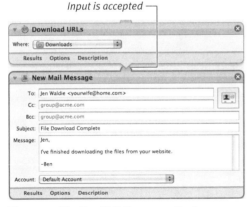

Figure 4.59 The New Mail Message action is configured to accept its input.

To tell an action to accept its input:

◆ Select the action in the workflow area and choose Action > Accept Input (**Figure 4.57**).

or

While holding down the Control key, click the action's title bar to display the contextual menu and choose Accept Input (**Figure 4.58**).

Automator links the action to the preceding action in the workflow again, visually indicating that it now accepts input again (**Figure 4.59**).

Viewing Action Results as a Workflow Runs

As a workflow runs within Automator, you may want to monitor the results of each action. Doing so lets you make sure that the correct information passes from action to action. As Chapter 9, "Troubleshooting," explains, this can be a valuable way to determine the cause of any problems you may encounter.

To view an action's result:

1. Select an action within the workflow.

2. Click the Results button at the bottom of the action (**Figure 4.60**).

   or

   Choose Action > Show Results (**Figure 4.61**).

   or

   Press ⌘K.

   The action expands to display a results area (**Figure 4.62**).

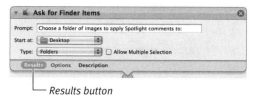

Results button

Figure 4.60 Click the Results button at the bottom of an action to display the action's results when the workflow runs.

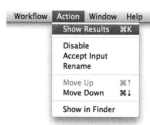

Figure 4.61 Choosing Show Results from the Action menu displays the selected action's results when the workflow runs.

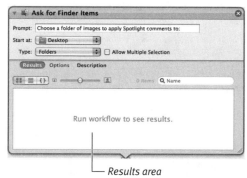

Results area

Figure 4.62 The results area of an expanded action, ready to show its results when the workflow runs.

Interpreting Action Results

Results vary from action to action. Some results, such as files and folders, iPhoto items, and iTunes songs, may be easy to interpret. Others, however, may be more difficult. Take your time, and do your best to make sense of them.

Start by viewing action results as icons. In many cases, you'll see previews, such as iPhoto image thumbnails. If no icons are displayed or if they all look the same, try list view. Here, you may find a bit more information, such as the full paths of files and folders.

View the results in list view as a last resort, however. Often, list view will display results as AppleScript code, which may not make a whole lot of sense if you don't know AppleScript.

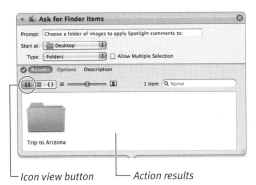

— Icon view button   — Action results

Figure 4.63 By default, action results are displayed as icons.

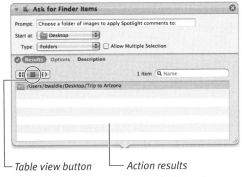

— Table view button   — Action results

Figure 4.64 Choosing to view an action's results as a table.

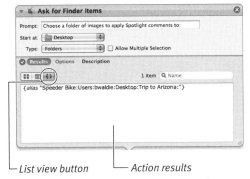

— List view button   — Action results

Figure 4.65 Choosing to view an action's results as a list.

3. Run the workflow.

As the workflow runs, the results area displays the results of the action (**Figure 4.63**).

By default, action results are displayed as icons. You can, however, view action results as a table or list. To change the view, click one of the view icons above the result area (**Figures 4.63, 4.64,** and **4.65**).

✔ Tip

■ Not all actions can display their results as icons. If you don't see anything listed when viewing an action's results as icons, try selecting another view.

TYPES OF
WORKFLOWS

Automator workflows are pretty versatile, as you know by now. They can be built and run within Automator, saved as Workflow files for later use, and even saved as stand-alone Applications. Although these methods are certainly useful in a variety of scenarios, Automator allows you to create additional types of workflows that are even more flexible and powerful. Workflows can be built as plug-ins for other applications or even for the operating system.

Workflow plug-ins can run in a more efficient or unique manner than a Workflow file or Application. It's like a way of adding your own features to the applications on your machine. For example, you can create a Service workflow, a plug-in for Mac OS X's system-wide Services architecture. Then you can run the workflow from a contextual menu to process selected text in an application such as Mail or TextEdit. Or, you can create an iCal Alarm workflow, which can be run by an iCal event at scheduled intervals, such as at night or while you're at lunch. You can even create a plug-in that runs anytime a file is added to a specified folder.

Chapter 3, "Workflow Basics," briefly covered some of the common steps involved in building, saving, and opening workflows. This chapter gets much more specific. You'll learn more about creating, saving, and running Workflow files and Applications, as well as the other types of workflows Automator supports—Services, Folder Actions, Print Plugins, iCal Alarms, and Image Capture Plugins. For each type of workflow discussed, step-by-step instructions walk you through the process of creating a simple example workflow to get you started.

Workflow Files

Workflow files (**Figure 5.1**) have been discussed to some extent throughout this text. This section serves as a recap, although it brings together the concepts discussed so far, making them a bit more cohesive.

Think of a Workflow file as a document file, such as a Microsoft Word document. Once saved, you can open a Workflow file in Automator, make changes to it, resave it, and close it. You can also run it within Automator.

Building a Workflow file

Imagine you're preparing to send out holiday cards to some of your closest business associates. Although you have their mailing addresses entered in Address Book, it is easiest to see them together in a single list.

This example workflow gets a list of selected recipients in Address Book, extracts their names and addresses, and inserts them into a new TextEdit document.

Actions used:

◆ Get Selected Address Book Items

◆ Get Contact Information

◆ New TextEdit Document

To build the workflow:

1. Create a new workflow. When the template selection panel appears, choose Workflow, and then click Choose (**Figure 5.2**).

   Automator creates an empty workflow window for you.

Figure 5.1 A Workflow file.

Figure 5.2 Creating a new Workflow file.

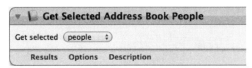

Figure 5.3 The Get Selected Address Book Items action's title changes to reflect the type of items it retrieves.

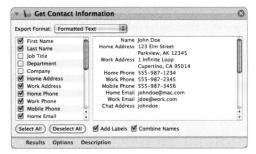

Figure 5.4 The Get Contact Information action as it appears when added to a workflow.

Figure 5.5 The Get Contact Information action configured to retrieve specific content fields.

Figure 5.6 The New TextEdit Document action has no modifiable settings.

2. From the Contacts category, drag the Get Selected Address Book Items action to the workflow area.

When the action's interface appears, its title changes to Get Selected Address Book People because it's configured to get people by default (**Figure 5.3**).

3. With the Contacts category still selected, drag the Get Contact Information action to the end of the workflow area (**Figure 5.4**).

4. Configure the Get Contact Information action's settings. Verify that the Export Format pop-up menu is set to Formatted Text. In the list of fields, select only the First Name, Last Name, and Work Address fields. Make sure the Add Labels checkbox is not selected and that the Combine Names checkbox is selected (**Figure 5.5**).

5. From the Text category, locate the New TextEdit Document action and add it to the workflow (**Figure 5.6**).

✔ Tip

■ Chapter 4, "Working with Actions," explains in detail how to locate an action and add it to a workflow.

Running a Workflow file

Generally, Workflow files are run within Automator, and that's what you'll do for this example. Some third-party applications also have the ability to run Workflow files. The Microsoft Office 2008 applications (Entourage, Excel, PowerPoint, and Word), for example, include script menus that can run Automator Workflow files.

✔ Tip

■ The system-wide Script menu that's built into Mac OS X (see the "Script Menu" section at the end of this chapter) can also run Workflow files.

To run the workflow:

1. Launch Address Book and select a few people to process (**Figure 5.7**).

2. Bring Automator back to the front.

3. Choose Workflow > Run (**Figure 5.8**).

   or

   Click the Run button in the workflow window toolbar (**Figure 5.9**).

   or

   Press ⌃ ⌘ R.

   The workflow runs. The names and addresses of the selected Address Book people are retrieved and inserted into a new TextEdit document (**Figure 5.10**).

Figure 5.7 Selecting some close business associates in Address Book.

Figure 5.8 Running the current workflow from the menu bar.

Figure 5.9 Running the workflow from the toolbar.

Figure 5.10 A TextEdit document contains the contact information retrieved by your workflow.

Figure 5.11 Saving a workflow.

Figure 5.12 Saving a workflow with a new name or in a new location.

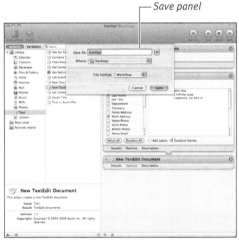

Figure 5.13 When you save a Workflow file, Automator displays the Save panel.

Saving and opening a Workflow file

Whenever you create a workflow, even if it's a quick one you only intend to use once, it's a good idea to save it. By doing so, you can reference it again in the future should the need ever arise. Believe me, referencing old workflows can come in handy when building new ones, and they provide a great jumping-off point. Also, even though you may not intend to use a workflow again, you never know what the future may bring. Archiving the workflow might just save you precious time later.

To save the workflow:

1. Choose File > Save (**Figure 5.11**) or press ⌃ ⌘ S.

   or

   If you need to save an existing workflow in the future using a new name or in a new location, choose File > Save As (**Figure 5.12**) or press ⇧ Shift ⌃ ⌘ S. You can do this to avoid overwriting your existing workflow.

   Automator displays the Save panel attached to the workflow window (**Figure 5.13**).

   continues on next page

WORKFLOW FILES

2. In the panel's Save As text field, type Build Address List (**Figure 5.14**).

3. From the Where pop-up menu, choose where you want to save the workflow.

4. Verify that the File Format pop-up menu is set to Workflow (**Figure 5.15**).

5. Click Save.

Automator saves the workflow as a Workflow file (**Figure 5.16**). You can now store it somewhere on your Mac for later use or send it to a friend.

✔ Tip

■ If you decide later that you want to convert your Workflow file to an Application, no problem. Just open it in Automator, choose File > Save As, and change the File Format pop-up menu to Application.

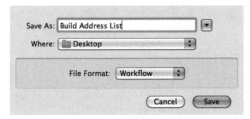

Figure 5.14 Enter a name for the Workflow file into the Save As field and choose a destination folder.

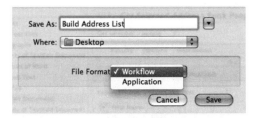

Figure 5.15 When saving a Workflow file, verify that the File Format pop-up menu is set to Workflow.

Figure 5.16 A saved Workflow file.

WORKFLOW FILES

Figure 5.17 Open a workflow by choosing File > Open.

Open Workflow button

Figure 5.18 Workflows can also be opened from the template selection panel.

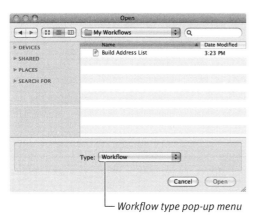

Workflow type pop-up menu

Figure 5.19 Set the Type pop-up menu in the Open window to allow you to choose a Workflow file.

To open the workflow:

1. Within Automator, choose File > Open (**Figure 5.17**).

   or

   Press ⌘O.

   or

   Create a new workflow window, and click the Open an Existing Workflow button in the template selection panel (**Figure 5.18**).

   The Open dialog appears.

2. In the Open dialog, set the Type pop-up menu to either Workflow or All.

3. Locate the Workflow file and click Open (**Figure 5.19**).

   The Workflow file opens in Automator. You can now modify the workflow, if desired, by inserting new actions, removing actions, or modifying action settings. When you're done, remember to resave the workflow (press ⌘S).

✔ Tip

■ You can also open a Workflow file by double-clicking it in the Finder or dragging it onto the Automator icon in your Dock.

WORKFLOW FILES

Workflow Applications

By now you know that Automator can save workflows as Applications (**Figure 5.20**). A workflow saved in this way works like any other application on your Mac. You launch it, and it runs by itself. You don't even need to launch Automator.

Figure 5.20 A workflow Application.

Building and saving a workflow Application

The Mac OS X Finder makes it easy to compress files or folders as .zip archives. To do so, just select a file or folder, and choose File > Compress from the menu bar (**Figure 5.21**). Once you've created an archive, you can send it as an email attachment by simply dragging it to the Mail icon in the Dock.

Figure 5.21 Compressing a file or folder in the Finder is as easy as selecting from a menu.

Application button

Figure 5.22 Creating a new workflow Application.

Header area

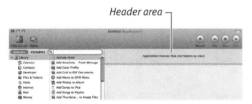

Figure 5.23 The header bar in a workflow Application lets you know that the workflow receives files and folders as input.

Indication that the action receives input

Figure 5.24 The Ask for Finder Items action when added to the workflow Application.

With Automator, you can turn this two-step process into a single step by creating a workflow Application that compresses a specified file or folder and attaches it to a new outgoing message in Mail.

Actions used:

◆ Ask for Finder Items

◆ Create Archive

◆ New Mail Message

To build the workflow:

1. Create a new workflow. In the template selection panel, click Application, and then click Choose (**Figure 5.22**).

   A new workflow window appears, and its header area indicates that the Application receives files and folders as input (**Figure 5.23**). You'll get to file and folder input handling shortly. For now, you'll configure the Application to prompt you to choose a file or folder to process.

2. Click the Files & Folders category in the action library. Select Ask for Finder Items, and drag it to the workflow area (**Figure 5.24**).

continues on next page

WORKFLOW APPLICATIONS

3. With the Ask for Finder Items action selected in the workflow area, choose Action > Ignore Input (**Figure 5.25**).

4. Set the action's Type pop-up menu to allow you to choose Files and Folders when prompted. You don't need to change any other settings for this action (**Figure 5.26**).

5. Drag the Create Archive action to the end of the workflow from the Files & Folders category in the Library list.

6. Select the "Ignore unreadable items" checkbox in the Create Archive action's interface. You can leave all other action settings set to their default values (**Figure 5.27**).

Figure 5.25 Disabling input from being passed to the Ask for Finder Items action.

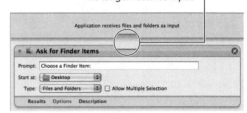

Figure 5.26 The configured Ask for Finder Items action no longer indicates that it receives input.

Figure 5.27 The properly configured Create Archive action.

WORKFLOW APPLICATIONS

Figure 5.28 The properly configured New Mail Message action.

Figure 5.29 The completed workflow Application.

Figure 5.30 A workflow Application displays an alert when run in Automator if the first action doesn't accept files and folders as input.

7. From the Mail category, locate the New Mail Message action, and add it to the end of the workflow. No additional configuration of this action is necessary (**Figure 5.28**).

The workflow is complete and is ready to be saved (**Figure 5.29**).

✔ Tips

■ Normally, it's a good idea to run a workflow in Automator before testing it externally to ensure it behaves as expected.

■ If you don't set the Ask for Finder Items action to ignore its input and you then try running the workflow in Automator, you'll see a warning indicating that the workflow expects files and folders as input (**Figure 5.30**).

To save the workflow:

1. Choose File > Save or press ⌃⌘S.

  or

  To save an existing Application using a new name or in a new location, choose File > Save As or press ⇧Shift⌃⌘S.

  Automator displays the Save panel attached to the workflow window.

2. In the panel's Save As text field, type Compress and Email.

3. From the Where pop-up menu, choose the folder in which you want to save the workflow.

4. Verify that the File Format pop-up menu is set to Application (**Figure 5.31**).

5. Click Save.

  Automator saves the workflow as a workflow Application (**Figure 5.32**). You can now run the workflow, send it to a friend, or file it on your Mac for later use.

✔ Tip

■ As you may recall, Workflow files can be saved as Applications. Likewise, Applications can be just as easily saved as Workflow files. Open the Application in Automator, choose File > Save As, and set the File Format pop-up menu in the Save panel to Workflow.

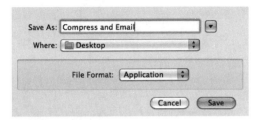

Figure 5.31 Automator's Save panel when saving a workflow as an Application.

Figure 5.32 A saved workflow Application.

Figure 5.33 An Automator workflow Application in the Applications folder.

Figure 5.34 Choosing an item to process with the workflow Application.

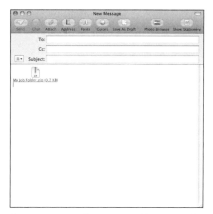

Figure 5.35 A Mail message with a .zip archive attachment.

Workflow activity indicator

Figure 5.36 The menu bar indicates when a workflow Application runs.

Running a workflow Application

A workflow Application behaves like any other Mac OS X application, and Automator doesn't need to be running to use it. You can move a workflow Application to, and run it from, anywhere on your Mac, such as the Applications or Documents folder or even your desktop (**Figure 5.33**).

Like other applications, workflow Applications can also be added to your Dock, added to the sidebar or toolbar of Finder windows, or simply launched by double-clicking on them.

To run the workflow:

1. Double-click the workflow Application in the Finder.

The workflow launches and begins running.

2. When prompted, select a file or folder to process. Then click Choose (**Figure 5.34**).

The workflow retrieves the chosen file or folder, compresses it into a .zip archive on your desktop, and attaches it to a new message in Mail (**Figure 5.35**).

What you see when the workflow runs:

◆ As the workflow Application runs, the menu bar displays a ✿ icon (**Figure 5.36**). If the workflow runs quickly, this icon may only appear briefly or you may not notice it at all.

◆ The workflow Application appears as a launched application in the Dock (**Figure 5.37**).

Figure 5.37 Workflow Applications appear in the Dock while running.

Quitting a workflow Application

There may be a time when you decide you need to cancel a workflow Application while it's running. For example, the workflow might be taking too long to run and you don't want to wait for it to complete, or you might have inadvertently launched the incorrect Application and need to stop it before it gets too far.

To quit a running workflow Application:

◆ Click the ⚙ icon in the menu bar and choose Stop and the Application's name (**Figure 5.38**).

    or

◆ Bring the Application to the front and choose Quit NewApplication from the Application's menu in the menu bar (**Figure 5.39**).

✔ Tip

■ The name NewApplication in the Application menu of a workflow Application is likely a bug and should really indicate the name of the Application.

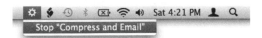

Figure 5.38 It's easy to stop a running workflow Application from the menu bar.

Figure 5.39 Quitting a workflow Application from the Application's menu.

WORKFLOW APPLICATIONS

Figure 5.40 Disabling an action from the menu bar.

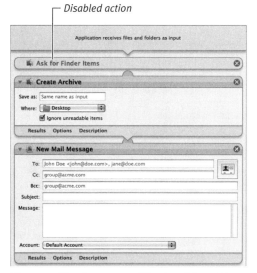

Figure 5.41 The Compress and Send workflow with a disabled Ask for Finder Items action.

Processing files and folders with a workflow Application

One of the most useful features of workflow Applications is that they are automatically saved as drag-and-drop applications, making it super easy to process files and folders. Simply drop some files or folders onto your workflow, and they are automatically passed as input to the first action for processing.

The first action in the Compress and Send workflow asks you to choose a file or folder to process. Because you've saved the workflow as an Application, however, you can simply drag a file or folder onto the Application to begin processing. Therefore, the Ask for Finder Items action is not necessary.

To prepare the workflow:

1. With the Compress and Send workflow Application opened in Automator, select the Ask for Finder Items action and choose Action > Disable (**Figure 5.40**). The Ask for Finder Items action should now appear grayed out, and its interface should be hidden (**Figure 5.41**).

2. Save the modified workflow (press ⌃ ⌘ S).

WORKFLOW APPLICATIONS

111

✔ Tips

■ With the Ask for Finder Items action disabled, any files or folders received as input to the workflow go directly to the Create Archive action.

■ Don't forget to check the description area of the first action in a workflow Application and make sure it accepts files and folders as input. Otherwise, the workflow won't be able to process dropped files and folders.

■ When building a drag-and-drop workflow Application, be sure not to include a Get Specified Finder Items or Get Selected Finder Items action at the beginning of the workflow. Otherwise, dropped items may be processed by the workflow twice!

To process files or folders:

◆ Drag and drop the files and folders you want to process onto the workflow Application (**Figure 5.42**).

The dropped files and folders are passed as input to the first action in the workflow Application. If the first action accepts files and folders, the dropped items are processed and you're off and rolling.

Figure 5.42 Drag and drop files and folders onto workflow Applications to begin processing them.

WORKFLOW APPLICATIONS

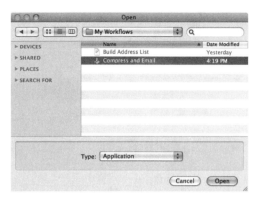

Figure 5.43 Opening a workflow Application.

Editing a workflow Application

The process for editing a workflow Application is a bit different than that for a Workflow file. Double-clicking on a Workflow file opens it in Automator, whereas double-clicking a workflow Application causes it to run. Therefore, you need to instruct Automator to open the Application.

To open a workflow Application:

1. In Automator, choose File > Open.

or

Press ⌃ ⌘ O.

or

Create a new workflow window, and click the Open an Existing Workflow button in the template selection panel.

An Open dialog is displayed, allowing you to choose a workflow.

2. In the Open dialog, set the Type pop-up menu to either Application or All. Setting it to Application ensures that you're only able to select workflows that are saved as Applications.

3. Locate the Application and click Open (**Figure 5.43**).

The workflow Application opens in Automator and is ready for editing.

✔ Tip

■ You can also open a workflow Application by dragging it from the Finder onto the Automator icon in your Dock.

WORKFLOW APPLICATIONS

113

Services

If you're an avid Mac OS X user, you may be familiar with Services, a powerful though fairly underutilized feature of the operating system. Services offer a way for applications to share their useful and unique features with other applications throughout the operating system.

For example, the Mail application "broadcasts" its ability to send an email message as a Service. When you're in another application, such as TextEdit, you can initiate this Service to quickly and easily generate a new message in Mail that contains the currently selected text. The application that provides the text is completely isolated from Mail, and it doesn't need to know anything about how to generate an email message. It simply passes the selected text to the Service, which handles the rest (**Figures 5.44** and **5.45**).

Figure 5.45 An email message containing selected text, created via a Service.

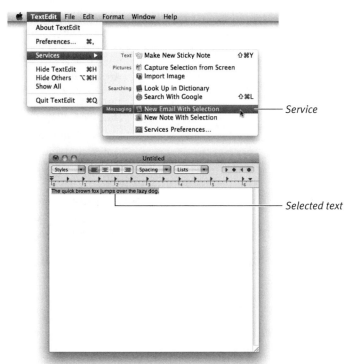

Figure 5.44 Triggering a Service built into Mac OS X to create a new email containing selected text.

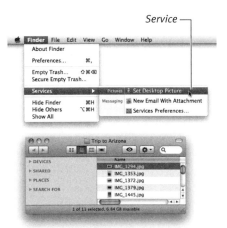

Figure 5.46 In most applications, Services can be run from the Services submenu in the application menu.

Figure 5.47 Some applications provide contextual menu access to Services.

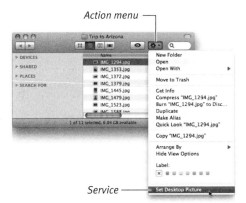

Figure 5.48 The Finder contains an Action menu, which provides access to Services.

Accessing Services

Services can be triggered in Mac OS X in several ways:

◆ **Services menu.** Most applications provide access to Services through a Services submenu in the application menu (**Figure 5.46**).

◆ **Contextual menus.** Many applications allow you to run Services from contextual menus. Hold down [Control] and click on some text or a file to display a contextual menu (**Figure 5.47**).

◆ **Custom access.** Some applications allow you to run Services in other, more integrated ways. For example, the Finder includes an Action menu, which lists Services (**Figure 5.48**).

◆ **Keyboard shortcuts.** Services can even be assigned keyboard shortcuts—which you can customize, if desired—making it even easier to trigger them (**Figure 5.49**).

Figure 5.49 Some Services can be run using keyboard shortcuts.

SERVICES

In Snow Leopard, Services are contextual. That is, they are enabled or disabled based on your current environment. For example, some Services are accessible only when you're in a specific application, whereas others are accessible in all applications. Services that have the ability to process data are accessible only when the appropriate type of data is selected. For example, a Service that processes text appears when text is selected, whereas a Service that processes image files only appears when image files are selected. Services irrelevant to the current environment are automatically hidden from view, reducing the possibility for confusion or error.

Services are also customizable, and you have full control over the Services that are available on your Mac. You can enable or disable specific Services, based on your unique needs, using System Preferences, as you'll learn shortly.

✔ Tips

■ Lots of Services are built into Mac OS X. As you install new applications, some of those applications add even more.

■ Unfortunately, the iLife and iWork (iPhoto, iMovie, Keynote, etc.) applications, as well as Apple's Pro applications (Aperture, Final Cut Pro, Logic, etc.) don't provide integrated Services support via contextual menus or other built-in methods. Therefore, the only way you can trigger Services within these applications is from the Services menu in the application menu.

Service button

Figure 5.50 Creating a Service workflow.

Data to process — Target application

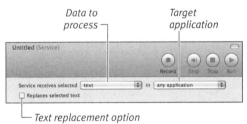

Text replacement option

Figure 5.51 A Service workflow provides configuration settings in the header bar above the workflow area.

Automator and Services

Snow Leopard introduces the ability to create your own custom Services with Automator. Simply build a new workflow, specify the type of content you want the workflow to process—such as text or image files—and choose whether the Service should be available in a specific application or in all applications. If your Service workflow processes text, you can also choose to replace the selected text with the processed text that's output by your workflow. After your Service has been saved, you can even assign it a keyboard shortcut, if desired.

In this section, you'll create two Service workflows that illustrate different ways of processing content. The first one processes text, and the second processes files.

Building, saving, and running a text processing Service workflow

The following example workflow processes selected text in an application. When triggered, it looks up a selected word or term in Mac OS X's dictionary and replaces the word or term with its definition. A Service like this might be useful to students for preparing a study sheet for an upcoming test.

Actions used:

◆ Get Definition of Word

To build the workflow:

1. Create a new workflow. When the template selection panel appears, select Service and click Choose (**Figure 5.50**).

   A new workflow window appears, and its header area includes some configuration options for the Service (**Figure 5.51**).

continues on next page

SERVICES

2. In the header area of the workflow, verify that the workflow is set to receive selected "text" from "any application" and that the "Replaces selected text" checkbox is selected (**Figure 5.52**).

Figure 5.52 Configuring a Service workflow to process selected text in any application.

3. From the Text category in the Library list, locate the Get Definition of Word action and drag it to the workflow. No additional configuration of this action is required (**Figure 5.53**).

That's it. The workflow is complete, and it's ready to be saved and tested in an application.

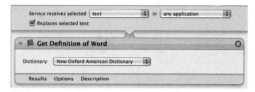

Figure 5.53 A Service workflow that looks up the definition of a word or term received as input.

✔ Tips

■ When building a Service workflow that processes text, make sure that the first action in the workflow accepts text as input.

■ When building a Service workflow that replaces selected text, make sure that the last action in the workflow produces text as its result.

Selectively Processing Text

Service workflows that process text can be made even more selective. They can actually be configured to process specific kinds of text. Mac OS X's data detection capabilities analyze selected text in an application and only allow your workflow to be run as a Service when appropriate.

To enable this functionality, just choose the desired kind of text you want the workflow to process from the pop-up menu in the workflow's header area (**Figure 5.54**). Options include:

◆ Text (i.e., any text)

◆ URLs

◆ Addresses

◆ Phone numbers

◆ Dates

◆ Email addresses

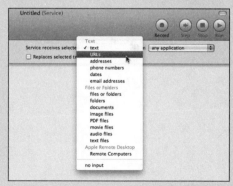

Figure 5.54 Service workflows can be configured to process specific kinds of text, such as URLs or email addresses.

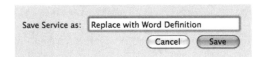

Figure 5.55 When saving a Service workflow, you only specify a name for the Service. Automator handles the rest.

To save the workflow:

1. Choose File > Save or press ⌃ ⌘ S.

   or

   To save an existing Service using a new name, choose File > Save As or press ⇧Shift ⌃ ⌘ S.

   Automator displays a Save panel attached to the workflow window. This Save panel is a bit different than that of a Workflow file or an Application. Rather than specifying an output location, you can only specify a name for the Service workflow.

2. In the panel's "Save Service as" text field, type Replace with Word Definition (**Figure 5.55**).

3. Click Save.

   Automator saves the workflow as a Service and installs it into the proper location on your machine automatically. You can now run the Service anytime you have selected text in an application that provides access to Services.

SERVICES

To run the workflow:

1. Launch TextEdit, create a new document, type and select a word or term you'd like to define, such as the term Steve Jobs (**Figure 5.56**).

2. Choose TextEdit > Services > Replace with Word Definition (**Figure 5.57**).

   or

   While holding down ⌃Control, click the selected text and choose Replace with Word Definition from TextEdit's contextual menu (**Figure 5.58**).

   The workflow runs, and the selected word or term is replaced with its definition (**Figure 5.59**).

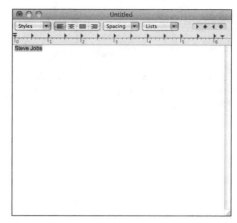

Figure 5.56 Selecting a term to define in a TextEdit document.

Figure 5.57 Triggering the Replace with Word Definition Service workflow from the Services menu.

Figure 5.58 Triggering the Replace with Word Definition Service workflow from a contextual menu.

Figure 5.59 The Service workflow replaces the selected word or term with its definition.

120

Figure 5.60 Stopping a Service workflow from the menu bar.

What you see when the workflow runs:

◆ As a Service workflow runs, the menu bar displays a ⚙ icon. If the workflow runs quickly, this icon may only appear briefly, in some cases, even too briefly to see.

To stop the running Service workflow:

◆ While the Service workflow is running, click the ⚙ icon in the menu bar and choose Stop "Replace with Word Definition" (**Figure 5.60**).

Building, saving, and running a file processing Service workflow

Processing files is just as easy as processing text. The following example workflow copies selected image files to the desktop to preserve the originals, and then converts them to a different type that is specified at runtime. For example, you might use this workflow to convert JPEG images to TIFF format.

Actions used:

◆ Copy Finder Items

◆ Change Type of Images

To build the workflow:

1. Create a new workflow. In the template selection panel, select Service and click Choose.

   A new workflow window appears with Services configuration options in the header area.

2. In the header area of the workflow, set the pop-up menus, respectively, to receive "image files" from the Finder (**Figure 5.61**).

3. Click the Files & Folders category in the library, and drag the Copy Finder Items action to the workflow. You don't need to modify its settings. By default, it copies items to the desktop (**Figure 5.62**).

4. From the Photos category, drag the Change Type of Images action to the workflow area (**Figure 5.63**).

5. Click Options at the bottom of the action, and select "Show this action when the workflow runs" (**Figure 5.64**).

   When your workflow runs, this action's interface is displayed, allowing you to choose the desired type of image on the fly.

The workflow is done (**Figure 5.65**).

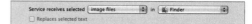

Figure 5.61 A Service workflow configured to receive image files from the Finder.

Figure 5.62 The Copy Finder Items action makes sure your original images stay safe.

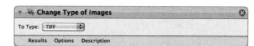

Figure 5.63 The Change Type of Images action converts images from one type to another.

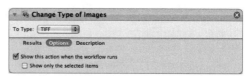

Figure 5.64 Configuring the Change Type of Images action to display its interface allows you to choose the desired type at runtime.

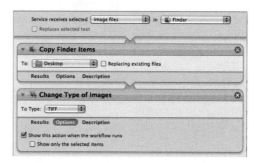

Figure 5.65 The completed file processing Service workflow.

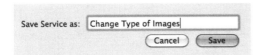

Figure 5.66 Saving the Change Type of Images Service workflow.

To save the workflow:

1. Choose File > Save or press ⌃ ⌘ S.

   or

   To save an existing Service using a new name, choose File > Save As or press ⇧ Shift ⌃ ⌘ S.

   Automator displays the Save panel attached to the workflow.

2. In the "Save Service as" text field, type Change Type of Images (**Figure 5.66**).

3. Click Save.

   Automator saves the Service and installs it for you.

Selectively Processing Files or Folders

Like text, you can configure a Service workflow to process specific kinds of files and folders. Once this is done, the Service can be run only on appropriate files (Figure 5.54). Available kinds of files or folders include:

◆ File or folders (i.e., any files or folders)

◆ Folders (no files)

◆ Documents

◆ Image files

◆ PDF files

◆ Movie files

◆ Audio files

◆ Text files

To run the workflow:

1. Bring the Finder to the front. Then locate and select some image files.

2. Choose Finder > Services > Change Type of Images (**Figure 5.67**).

    or

    While holding down (Control), click the selected images and choose Change Type of Images from the contextual menu (**Figure 5.68**).

    or

    Choose Change Type of Images from the Action menu in the toolbar of the window containing the images (**Figure 5.69**).

    The workflow begins running, and the selected image files are passed to the first action in the workflow as input—much like dropping files onto a workflow application. The images are first copied

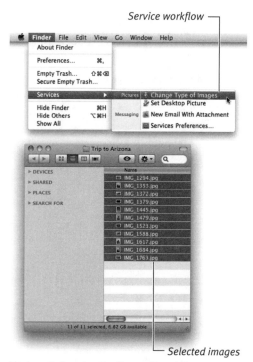

Service workflow

Selected images

Figure 5.67 Running the Change Type of Images workflow from the Services menu.

Service workflow

Figure 5.68 Running the Change Type of Images workflow from the Finder's contextual menu.

Service workflow

Figure 5.69 Running the Change Type of Images workflow from the Finder window's Action menu.

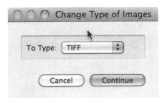

Figure 5.70 The Change Type of Images action's interface displays at runtime.

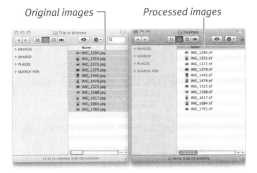

Original images — *Processed images*

Figure 5.71 Original images (JPEGs) and images produced by the Change Type of Images Service workflow (TIFFs).

to the desktop. Then the Change Type of Images action's window appears, allowing you to choose the desired image type (**Figure 5.70**).

3. Choose the desired type of images from the To Type pop-up menu. For example, if your images are JPEGs, you could choose TIFF.

4. Click Continue.

The copied images on your desktop are converted to the specified type, and you now have two sets of images, the originals and a new set (**Figure 5.71**). You're done. It's that easy.

✔ Tips

■ Don't worry about losing your original images. Remember, the Copy Finder Items action copies the images to your desktop before the images are processed.

■ You can find dozens of useful downloadable Service workflows at www.macosxautomation.com/services/.

SERVICES

Other Types of Services

A Service workflow doesn't have to process text or files or folders. A Service workflow can also run without processing any input data. To configure a Service to behave in this manner, set the first pop-up menu in the header area to process "no input" (**Figure 5.72**). When the Service is triggered, it simply runs without acting on the selected data.

— No input

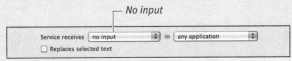

Figure 5.72 Service workflows can be configured to require no input.

For Apple Remote Desktop users, Service workflows can even be built to process Remote Computers, allowing you to create Services that automate remote administrative tasks (**Figure 5.73**).

— Remote Computers

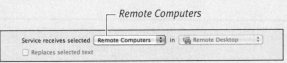

Figure 5.73 Service workflows can be configured to process Remote Computers in Apple Remote Desktop.

Editing a Service Workflow

Like other types of workflows, you can open Service workflows and edit them.

To open a Service workflow:

1. In Automator, choose File > Open.

   or

   Press ⌃ ⌘ O.

   or

   Create a new workflow window, and click the Open an Existing Workflow button in the template selection panel.

   An Open window appears, prompting you to select a workflow.

2. Set the Type pop-up menu to either Service or All.

3. Locate the desired Service and click Open (**Figure 5.74**).

   The Service opens in Automator and is ready for editing.

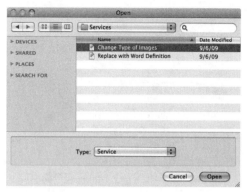

Figure 5.74 Opening a saved Service workflow.

What About Finder Plug-ins?

If you've used Automator in Mac OS X 10.4 Tiger or 10.5 Leopard, recall that Automator allowed you to save workflows as Finder plug-ins. These plug-ins appeared in the Finder's contextual menu and could be run to process selected files and folders.

In Snow Leopard, Finder plug-ins have been replaced by Service workflows. This means that if you have existing Finder plug-in workflows, you won't see them in the Finder's contextual menu anymore. To get them back, you'll need to re-create them as Service workflows.

Actually, you can still open your existing Finder plug-ins in Automator. You'll find them in the ~/Library/Workflows/Applications/Finder folder in your home folder. Once opened, you can then merge them into new Service workflows. See "Converting Workflow Types," later in this chapter to learn how to do this.

SERVICES

✔ Tips

- Service workflows reside in the ~/Library/Services directory (**Figure 5.75**). When you set the Type pop-up menu in the Open dialog to Service, Automator automatically displays the contents of this folder.

- A tilde (~) at the beginning of a folder path means that the folder resides in your home (i.e., user) directory.

- At times, you may want to open an existing Service workflow, change its input type, such as from text to URLs, and then resave it. If you do this but the change doesn't appear to take effect in the Services menu, try performing a Save As instead and replacing the previous version of the workflow with the modified version.

Figure 5.75 Service workflows are stored in the ~/Library/Services folder.

Configuring Service workflows

As you build more workflows and install more applications, your list of Services will likely continue to grow considerably, and you'll need a way to manage them.

For example, you may not want or need all Services to be active on your machine at once. To help, Mac OS X allows you to enable or disable individual Services. A disabled Service no longer appears in the Services menu or other areas in which Services are triggered.

Mac OS X also allows you to assign keyboard shortcuts (i.e., key commands) to Services. Doing this to your commonly used Services can improve your workflow by reducing mouse clicks. Simply press the appropriate keys and the Service begins running.

Services are configured via the Keyboard settings in System Preferences.

To disable or enable a Service workflow:

1. From the Apple menu, choose System Preferences (**Figure 5.76**).

   The System Preferences application launches (**Figure 5.77**).

2. Click Keyboard.

   The keyboard settings are displayed (**Figure 5.78**).

Figure 5.76 Opening System Preferences via the Apple menu.

Keyboard settings

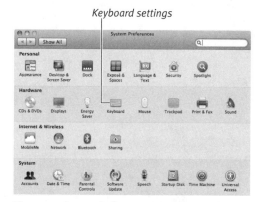

Figure 5.77 System Preferences provides access to loads of system-wide settings on your Mac.

Keyboard Shortcuts tab

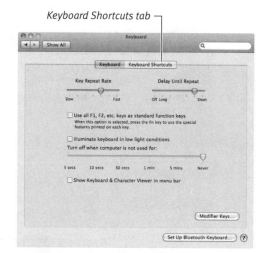

Figure 5.78 The keyboard settings area in System Preferences.

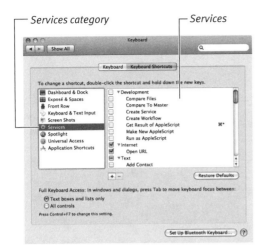

Services category   *Services*

Figure 5.79 Viewing settings for Services in the Keyboard area in System Preferences.

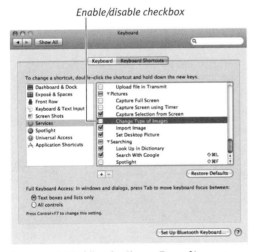

Enable/disable checkbox

Figure 5.80 Disabling the Change Type of Images Service.

3. Click the Keyboard Shortcuts tab if it's not already selected.

A list of global keyboard shortcuts organized into categories is displayed.

4. Click the Services category in the column on the left side of the window (**Figure 5.79**).

A list of Services is displayed.

5. Scroll through the list, and deselect a checkbox next to a Service to disable it (**Figure 5.80**).

The Service is disabled throughout the operating system. To enable it again, return to the Keyboard Shortcuts tab in the keyboard settings area in System Preferences, and select the Service's checkbox again.

✔ Tip

■ To remove a Service workflow entirely, go to ~/Library/Services and delete the workflow.

To assign a keyboard shortcut to a Service workflow:

1. In the Keyboard Shortcuts tab in the keyboard settings area in System Preferences, locate the desired Service.

2. Double-click the area immediately to the right of the Service's name.

3. Press the desired keyboard shortcut, such as [Control][Option]⌃⌘[C] (**Figure 5.81**).

   The shortcut is applied and now appears next to the Service in the Services menu (**Figure 5.82**).

Keyboard shortcut

Figure 5.81 Assigning a keyboard shortcut to a service.

Keyboard shortcut

Figure 5.82 A Service with a keyboard shortcut.

Managing Services

Services Manager (**Figure 5.83**), a third-party utility, makes it even easier to configure Services in Snow Leopard. Its concise interface provides a more organized hierarchy of Services than you'll find in System Preferences and even allows you to create your own custom groupings of frequently used Services.

Services Manager makes it easy to enable and disable Services, and add keyboard shortcuts. It also allows you to specify whether individual Services appear in contextual menus, as well as how many Services can be displayed in contextual menus—there's normally a limit.

You can download this useful utility from www.macosxautomation.com/services/servicesmanager/.

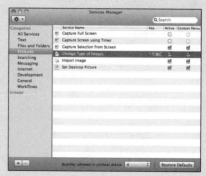

Figure 5.83 Services Manager, a third-party utility for managing Services in Mac OS X.

SERVICES

Folder Actions

Need to create an unattended watched folder workflow? It's simple. Just build an Automator workflow as a Folder Action and attach it to a specified folder. Once set up, there's no need for you to monitor the folder for incoming items. The workflow automatically runs whenever files or folders are added to the folder.

As I'm sure you can imagine, there are countless uses for such a workflow. For example, you could attach a Folder Action to your incoming fax folder to run whenever a new fax arrives. Or, you could create a Folder Action that alerts you whenever someone copies a file into your Public folder. The possibilities are virtually endless.

Building and saving a Folder Action workflow

In this section, you'll learn how to create a Folder Action workflow that runs whenever images are placed into a folder. Once triggered, it moves the detected images to the desktop and duplicates them into another folder to preserve the originals. It then converts the duplicate images to black and white.

Actions used:

◆ Move Finder Items

◆ New Folder

◆ Get Folder Contents

◆ Apply Quartz Composition Filter to Image Files

To build the workflow:

1. Create a new folder on your desktop and name it Conversion Input (**Figure 5.84**). This folder will be utilized by the workflow.

2. Bring Automator to the front and create a new workflow. When the template selection panel appears, choose to create a Folder Action. Then click Choose (**Figure 5.85**).

   A new workflow window appears, and its header area indicates that the Folder Action receives files and folders added to a folder, which you have yet to specify (**Figure 5.86**).

3. Choose Other from the pop-up menu in the header area.

   A window appears, and you are asked to select a folder.

Figure 5.84 A desktop folder ready to become a fully automated watched folder.

Conversion Input

Folder Action button ¬

Figure 5.85 Creating a Folder Action workflow.

Figure 5.86 A Folder Action workflow's header lets you know that the workflow receives files and folders as input.

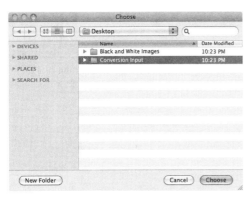

Figure 5.87 Choosing a watched folder for the Folder Action workflow.

Figure 5.88 The Folder Action workflow, configured to watch a specific folder.

Figure 5.89 The Move Finder Items action moves detected items out of the watched folder for processing.

Figure 5.90 The New Folder action creates an output folder for the processed image files.

Figure 5.91 The New Folder action's description shows that the action copies items passed as input into the new folder.

4. Locate the Conversion Input folder you created on the desktop in step 1. Then click Choose (**Figure 5.87**).

   The pop-up menu in the workflow's header area updates to show the chosen folder (**Figure 5.88**).

5. From the Files & Folders category in the Library list, drag the Move Finder Items action to the workflow area. You can leave it set to move items to the Desktop and not to replace existing items (**Figure 5.89**).

   This action moves detected items out of the attached folder, so they aren't accidentally detected by the workflow a second time.

6. Drag the New Folder action to the work-flow. Type Black and White Images into the Name field, and leave the Where pop-up set to create the folder on the Desktop (**Figure 5.90**).

   If you check the description of the New Folder action, you'll see that it copies files and folders it receives as input into the new folder. Therefore, an additional action isn't needed to duplicate the images into the new folder, because this happens automatically (**Figure 5.91**).

continues on next page

FOLDER ACTIONS

7. With the Files & Folders category still selected in the Library, drag the Get Folder Contents action to the end of the workflow (**Figure 5.92**).

This action is necessary because the result of the New Folder action is the newly created folder. What you want, however, is the contents of the newly created folder, not the folder itself.

8. Click the Photos category in the Library list. Locate the Apply Quartz Filter to Image Files action, and add it to the workflow.

When you do this, Automator displays a warning, which indicates that the action will change your image files when the workflow runs. The warning suggests inserting a Copy Finder Items action first to preserve the originals. The workflow already creates duplicates of your original images. So, this additional step is unnecessary, because it would just create yet another copy. Choose not to insert the Copy Finder Items action by clicking Don't Add (**Figure 5.93**).

The Apply Quartz Filter to Image Files action is added to the workflow. Set the action's pop-up menu to Black and White (**Figure 5.94**).

The Folder Action workflow is complete and is ready to be saved (**Figure 5.95**).

Figure 5.92 The Get Folder Contents action gets the image files from the newly created folder.

Figure 5.93 The Apply Quartz Filter to Image Files action warns you that it modifies your image files.

Figure 5.94 The Apply Quartz Filter to Image Files action converts your images to black and white during processing.

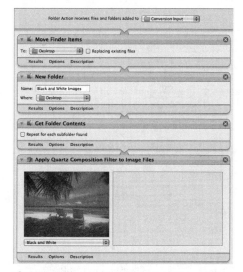

Figure 5.95 The completed Folder Action workflow ready to be saved.

Figure 5.96 Saving a Folder Action workflow.

✔ Tips

■ Make sure that your Folder Action workflow doesn't create or rename files in the attached folder. Otherwise, they'll be detected by the Folder Action and be processed by the workflow. This can create a vicious cycle and simply isn't a good idea.

■ To improve Folder Action performance, it's good practice to remove items from the watched folder immediately after processing.

■ Whenever modifying images or other files, especially in an irreversible way, it's best practice to work with duplicates of your originals. This way you can revert back to the originals should you need to do so. Just be sure not to create the duplicates in the watched folder.

To save the workflow:

1. Choose File > Save or press ⌃ ⌘ S.

   or

   To save an existing Folder Action using a new name, choose File > Save As or press ⇧Shift ⌃ ⌘ S.

   Automator displays a Save panel.

2. In the "Save Folder Action as" field, type Convert Images to Black and White (**Figure 5.96**).

3. Click Save.

   Automator saves the workflow as a Folder Action, installs it into the proper location on your machine, and attaches it to the folder you chose when you built the workflow.

FOLDER ACTIONS

135

Running a Folder Action workflow

Running a Folder Action workflow could not be easier.

To run the workflow:

◆ Select one or more images in the Finder, and drag them into the Conversion Input folder on the desktop (**Figure 5.97**).

After a second or two, the Automator workflow begins running. The images are moved to the desktop, duplicated into a new folder named Black and White Images—which the workflow creates—and converted to black and white (**Figure 5.98**).

✔ Tips

■ In Snow Leopard, Folder Actions try to wait for an item to finish writing to the attached folder before triggering. This is done by monitoring the size of the item until it remains unchanged for at least three seconds. In previous versions of Mac OS X, Folder Actions triggered immediately when an item appeared in the folder, causing problems if the item was still copying or saving.

■ A workflow very similar to the Convert Images example Folder Action in this section was used to prepare all the screen shots for this book as black and white TIFF images.

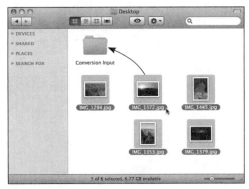

Figure 5.97 Select some image files, and drag them to the watched folder for processing.

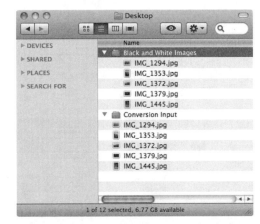

Figure 5.98 The original images move to the desktop, and the processed images appear in a new folder.

Figure 5.99 You can stop running a Folder Action workflow via the menu bar.

What you see when the workflow runs:

◆ As a Folder Action workflow runs, the menu bar displays a ✿ icon. If the workflow runs quickly, this icon may only appear briefly, in some cases, even too briefly to see.

To stop the running Folder Action workflow:

◆ While the Folder Action workflow is running, click the ✿ icon in the menu bar and choose Stop "Convert Images to Black and White" (**Figure 5.99**).

Folder Actions and AppleScript

Folder Actions can also be written in AppleScript, and doing so offers you some additional processing opportunities. Like an Automator-based Folder Action, an AppleScript can be written to run when items are placed into the attached folder. It can also, however, be written to run when items are removed from the attached folder, when the folder's window is opened, or when the folder's window is closed.

Editing a Folder Action

Folder Action workflows can be reopened and edited, if needed, just like other types of workflows.

To open a Folder Action workflow:

1. Within Automator, choose File > Open.

    or

    Press ⌃ ⌘ O.

    or

    Create a new workflow window, and click the Open an Existing Workflow button in the template selection panel.

2. In the Open dialog, set the Type pop-up menu to either Folder Action or All.

3. Locate the desired Folder Action and click Open (**Figure 5.100**).

    The Folder Action workflow opens in Automator and is ready for editing.

✔ Tip

■ Folder Action workflows reside in the ~/Library/Workflows/Applications/Folder Actions directory (**Figure 5.101**). When you set the Type pop-up menu in the Open dialog to Folder Action, Automator automatically displays the contents of this folder.

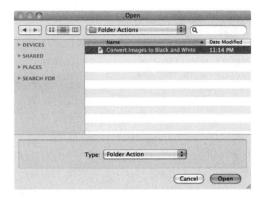

Figure 5.100 Opening an existing Folder Action workflow in Automator.

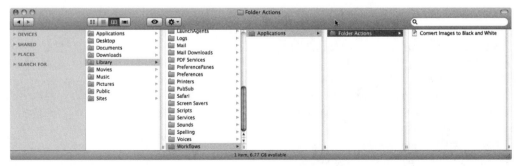

Figure 5.101 Folder Action workflows are saved in ~/Library/Workflows/Applications/Folder Actions.

FOLDER ACTIONS

Figure 5.102
You launch Folder Actions Setup from the Finder's contextual menu.

Figure 5.103 Folder Actions Setup allows you to manage your Folder Actions.

Figure 5.104
Sometimes, Folder Actions Setup prompts you to choose a script to attach.

Managing Folder Actions

The Folder Actions Setup application provides a central place to manage all the Folder Actions that are configured on your machine. Here, you can enable or disable Folder Actions, create new watched folders, and more.

To access Folder Actions Setup:

1. While holding the Control key, click on a folder to display the Finder's contextual menu.

2. Choose Folder Actions Setup from the contextual menu (**Figure 5.102**).

   The Folder Actions Setup application launches (**Figure 5.103**).

✔ Tips

- If you are prompted to choose a script to attach when Folder Actions Setup launches, you can simply click Cancel (**Figure 5.104**).

- The Folder Action Setup application is found in the /System/Library/CoreServices folder (**Figure 5.105**). You can launch it from there, if you prefer, rather than from the Finder's contextual menu.

- In Mac OS X 10.4 Tiger and 10.5 Leopard, Folder Actions Setup was found in /Applications/AppleScript. This folder no longer exists in Snow Leopard.

Figure 5.105 Folder Actions Setup is found in /System/Library/CoreServices on your Mac.

FOLDER ACTIONS

To disable or enable a Folder Action:

◆ In the left column of the Folder Actions Setup window, deselect the checkbox next to desired Folder Action (**Figure 5.106**).

The Folder Action is now disabled. To enable it again, select the Folder Action's checkbox in the left column of the window.

As you build more and more Folder Action workflows on your Mac, use these steps to enable or disable them as needed.

To disable or enable all Folder Actions:

◆ Deselect the Enable Folder Actions checkbox in the Folder Actions Setup application (**Figure 5.107**).

Folder Actions are disabled system-wide on your Mac. To enable them again, select the Enable Folder Actions checkbox in Folder Actions Setup.

To detach a Folder Action from a folder:

◆ In the left column of the Folder Actions Setup window, select the desired Folder Action and click the minus (–) button beneath the column.

Folder Actions Setup displays an alert panel asking you to confirm you really want to delete the Folder Action. Click OK (**Figure 5.108**).

The Folder Action is detached from its folder.

✔ Tip

■ If you want to actually delete a Folder Action workflow rather than just detaching it from its folder, go to the ~/Library/Workflows/Applications/Folder Actions folder, find the workflow, and move it to the trash.

Enable/disable individual Folder Action checkbox

Figure 5.106 Disabling an existing Folder Action.

Enable/disable all Folder Actions checkbox

Figure 5.107 Folder Actions can be disabled system-wide, if desired.

Figure 5.108 Folder Actions Setup warns you before removing a Folder Action.

Figure 5.109 Choosing a watched folder for a Folder Action.

Figure 5.110 Choosing a Folder Action to attach to a folder.

To attach an existing Folder Action to a new folder:

1. In the left column of the Folder Actions Setup window, click the plus (+) button beneath the column.

   A window appears, and you are prompted to choose a folder.

2. Locate the desired folder and click Open (**Figure 5.109**).

   The window disappears, and a new panel prompts you to choose a Folder Action to attach to the folder.

3. Select the desired Folder Action. Then click Attach (**Figure 5.110**).

   The window closes, and Folder Actions Setup indicates that the Folder Action is attached to the specified folder (**Figure 5.111**).

✔ Tip

■ This example uses an AppleScript-based Folder Action—add - new item alert. scpt—that's built into Mac OS X. Once configured, this Folder Action displays a message anytime a new item is detected in the attached folder (**Figure 5.112**).

Figure 5.111 A watched folder attached to a Folder Action.

Figure 5.112 The "add – new item alert.scpt" Folder Action notifies you when an item is added to the attached folder.

FOLDER ACTIONS

Print Plugins

You are probably already aware that you can convert any Mac OS X document to PDF format by selecting Save as PDF from the PDF pop-up menu at the bottom of the Print window. To further enhance your PDF processing capabilities, Automator allows you to create Print Plugins, which can also be run from this menu. When printing any document, in virtually any application in Mac OS X, simply choose the workflow to save the current document as a PDF and begin processing it with your workflow (**Figure 5.113**).

Building and saving a Print Plugin

As you may know, metadata, such as an author's name, copyright information, keywords, and more, may be embedded into PDF documents. This information can be useful for determining the source, content, or creator of a PDF.

For this example, you'll create a Print Plugin that can be triggered from the PDF pop-up menu in the Mac OS X Print window in any application. Once triggered, the workflow saves your document as a PDF, moves it to the desktop, names it using the current date, and adds specified metadata to it.

Actions used:

◆   Move Finder Items

◆   Rename Finder Items

◆   Set PDF Metadata

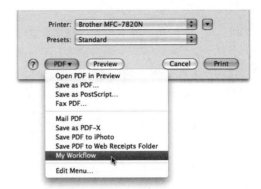

Figure 5.113 Automator workflows can be triggered from the Print window in Mac OS X.

Print Plugin button

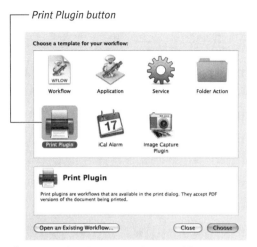

Figure 5.114 Creating a Print Plugin workflow.

Figure 5.115 The header area of a Print Plugin workflow.

Figure 5.116 The Rename Finder Items action warns you that the names of your files will be changed.

Add before names option

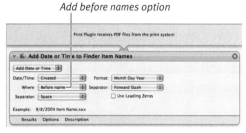

Figure 5.117 Set the Rename Finder Items action to add the current date before the file names.

To build the workflow:

1. In Automator, create a new workflow. When the template selection panel appears, choose to create a Print Plugin and click Choose (**Figure 5.114**).

   A new workflow window appears, and its header area indicates that the Print Plugin receives PDF files from the print system (**Figure 5.115**).

2. From the Files & Folders category, drag the Rename Finder Items action to the workflow area.

   Automator displays a warning, indicating that the action will change the names of your files in an irreversible way. The warning suggests inserting a Copy Finder Items action first to preserve the original names. This isn't necessary, since the workflow is processing a newly created PDF document, so click Don't Add to prevent the Copy Finder Items action from being added to the workflow (**Figure 5.116**).

   The Rename Finder Items action is added to the workflow. It's already configured to add the current date to the names of files. Simply change the Where pop-up menu to add the date before the name rather than after it (**Figure 5.117**).

continues on next page

PRINT PLUGINS

3. Drag the Move Finder Items action to the workflow area.

The action should already be set to move files to the Desktop, so no additional configuration is needed (**Figure 5.118**).

4. From the PDFs category, drag the Set PDF Metadata action to the workflow area.

5. Click the checkbox next to the Author text field, and enter your name. Then click the checkbox next to the Content Creator field, and enter some text, such as copyright information. If you'd like, you can enable other fields and enter default values into them too.

6. Click the Options button at the bottom of the action.

The action expands to display additional options.

7. Click "Show this action when the workflow runs" (**Figure 5.119**).

When the workflow runs, it displays the Set PDF Metadata action, enabling you to modify the text fields, enter keywords, and more.

The workflow is complete and ready to be saved (**Figure 5.120**).

✔ Tips

■ To insert the © symbol in text, press Option G.

■ Print Plugins process PDFs that are written into a hidden temporary folder on your Mac. So, it's a good idea to use the Move Finder Items action to move them somewhere useful during processing, such as the desktop or your Documents folder.

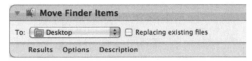

Figure 5.118 The Move Finder Items action moves the PDF to the desktop when the workflow runs.

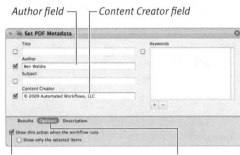

Author field ⎯ ⎯ *Content Creator field*

Show action when run checkbox   *Options button*

Figure 5.119 The Set PDF Metadata action, which contains some default values, displays its interface when the workflow runs.

Figure 5.120 The finished Create Dated PDF with Metadata workflow.

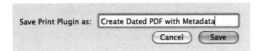

Figure 5.121 Saving a Print Plugin workflow.

To save the workflow:

1. Choose File > Save or press ⌃⌘S.

   or

   To save an existing Print Plugin using a new name, choose File > Save As or press ⇧Shift⌃⌘S.

   Automator displays the Save panel.

2. In the "Save Print Plugin as" field, type Create Dated PDF with Metadata (**Figure 5.121**).

3. Click Save.

   Automator saves the workflow as a Print Plugin and installs it into the proper location on your machine.

PRINT PLUGINS

Running a Print Plugin workflow

A saved Print Plugin workflow automatically appears in the PDF pop-up menu of the Mac OS X Print window whenever you print something.

To run the workflow:

1. Open a document to print, such as a TextEdit document. Or, if desired, you can simply use your opened Automator workflow.

2. Choose File > Print.

   or

   Press ⌃ ⌘ P.

   The Mac OS X Print window is displayed.

3. Choose Create Dated PDF with Metadata from the PDF pop-up menu in the bottom left of the Print window (**Figure 5.122**).

   The currently opened document is saved as a PDF to a temporary folder, and the Insert PDF Metadata Automator workflow runs and begins to process the PDF.

   The workflow first renames the PDF by appending a date prefix. Next, it moves the PDF to the desktop. Then it displays the Set PDF Metadata window.

4. Enter the desired information into the Set PDF Metadata window, such as a title for the PDF, a subject, and keywords.

5. Click Continue (**Figure 5.123**).

   The workflow appends the specified metadata to the PDF.

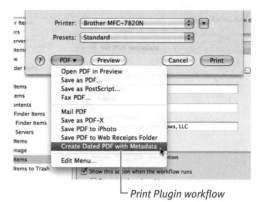

Print Plugin workflow

Figure 5.122 Running a Print Plugin workflow from the Mac OS X Print window.

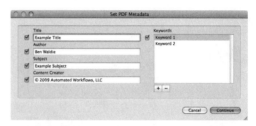

Figure 5.123 The Set PDF Metadata window allows you to modify metadata values at runtime.

9/8/2009 Create Dated P...adata.pdf

Figure 5.124 A dated PDF created by the Print Plugin workflow.

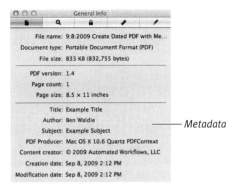

Figure 5.125 Viewing metadata for a PDF in Preview's Inspector palette.

You should now see a PDF on your desktop with a date prefix (**Figure 5.124**). To verify that the metadata was successfully applied, open the PDF in Preview and choose Tools > Show Inspector (or press ⌘⌥I) to display an information window. The information window should list the metadata values that you specified when the workflow ran (**Figure 5.125**).

What you see when the workflow runs:

◆ As a Print Plugin workflow runs, the menu bar displays a ☼ icon. If the workflow runs quickly, this icon may only appear briefly, in some cases, even too briefly to see.

To stop running the Print Plugin workflow:

◆ While the Print Plugin workflow is running, click the ☼ icon in the menu bar and choose Stop "Create Dated PDF with Metadata."

Editing a Print Plugin Workflow

Automator saves Print Plugin workflows as specially formatted workflow files into the ~/Library/PDF Services folder on your Mac (**Figure 5.126**).

To open the workflow:

1. Within Automator, choose File > Open.

   or

   Press ⌃ ⌘ O.

   or

   Create a new workflow window, and click the Open an Existing Workflow button in the template selection panel.

2. In the Open dialog, set the Type pop-up menu to either Print Plugin or All.

3. Locate the desired Print Plugin and click Open (**Figure 5.127**).

   The Print Plugin workflow opens in Automator and is ready for editing.

✔ Tips

- When you set the Type pop-up menu in the Open dialog to Print Plugin, Automator automatically displays the contents of the ~/Library/PDF Services folder.

- To delete or remove a Print Plugin, simply navigate to the ~/Library/PDF Services folder, locate the workflow, and move it to the trash or another folder. When you do this, the workflow no longer appears in the PDF pop-up menu at the bottom of the Print window.

Figure 5.126 Print Plugin workflows are saved into ~/Library/PDF Services.

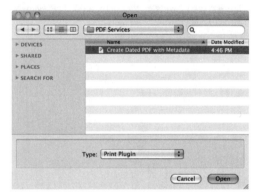

Figure 5.127 Opening a Print Plugin workflow.

PRINT PLUGINS

iCal Alarms

As you may recall from Chapter 2, "Building Simple Workflows," an Automator workflow can be saved as an iCal Alarm, enabling you to configure the workflow to run at a specific date and time. You can even set it to run on a repeating schedule, such as every day at midnight. In Chapter 2, you created an iCal Alarm that did just this—it sent birthday greetings via email every evening.

Building, saving, and running an iCal Alarm workflow

In this section, you'll create another iCal Alarm workflow. This workflow wakes you up by playing a specified iTunes playlist at a scheduled time in the morning, complete with iTunes visuals.

Actions used:

◆ Get Specified iTunes Items

◆ Play iTunes Playlist

◆ Start iTunes Visuals

To build the workflow:

1. Create a new workflow in Automator. When the template selection panel appears, choose iCal Alarm. Then click Choose (**Figure 5.128**).

   A new workflow window appears, and its header area indicates that the iCal Alarm is run when triggered by an event in iCal (**Figure 5.129**).

2. From the Music category in the Library list, drag the Get Specified iTunes Items action to the workflow (**Figure 5.130**).

continues on next page

iCal Alarm button

Figure 5.128 Creating an iCal Alarm workflow.

Figure 5.129 An iCal Alarm workflow's header lets you know that the workflow is run by an iCal event.

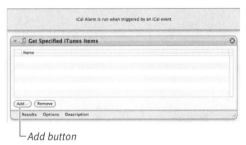

Add button

Figure 5.130 The Get Specified iTunes Items action as it appears when first added to a workflow.

iCAL ALARMS

149

3. Click the Add button at the bottom of the Get Specified iTunes Items action.

A panel is displayed, and you're asked to select an iTunes item.

4. Select a playlist, such as Top 25 Most Played, and click Add (**Figure 5.131**).

The selected playlist appears in the Get Specified iTunes Items action's interface (**Figure 5.132**).

5. Locate the Play iTunes Playlist action in the Library list, and drag it to the workflow. You don't need to change any settings in this action (**Figure 5.133**).

6. Add the Start iTunes Visuals action to the end of the workflow.

7. Select the "Full screen" checkbox in the Start iTunes Visuals action's interface (**Figure 5.134**).

This action displays some relaxing graphics to help you wake up when the playlist begins playing.

The workflow is complete (**Figure 5.135**). Now, it's time to save it.

Figure 5.131 Choose an iTunes Playlist to be used by the workflow.

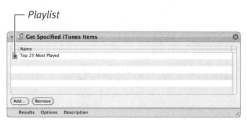

Figure 5.132 The Get Specified iTunes Items action includes the chosen playlist.

Figure 5.133 The Play iTunes Playlist action plays the specified playlist when the workflow runs.

Figure 5.134 The Start iTunes Visuals action enables full-screen visuals to accompany the music.

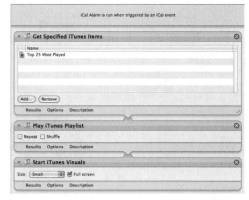

Figure 5.135 The complete iTunes Alarm Clock workflow.

Figure 5.136 Saving an iCal Alarm workflow.

Figure 5.137 When an iCal Alarm is saved, iCal launches, and a new event is created, configured to trigger the workflow.

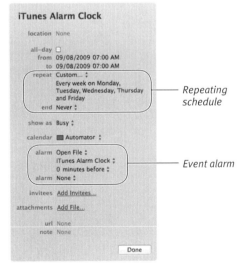

Repeating schedule

Event alarm

Figure 5.138 iCal Alarm events can be adjusted to run the workflow on a schedule, such as every weekday at 7 am.

To save the workflow:

1. Choose File > Save or press ⌃ ⌘ S.

   or

   To save an existing iCal Alarm using a new name in the future, choose File > Save As or press ⇧ Shift ⌃ ⌘ S.

   Automator displays a Save panel attached to the workflow window.

2. In the panel's "Save iCal Alarm as" text field, type iTunes Alarm Clock (**Figure 5.136**).

3. Click Save.

   Automator saves the workflow as an iCal Alarm and installs it into the proper location on your machine.

   Next, iCal launches, and a new event is created at the current date and time in a calendar named Automator. The event is configured to an alarm, which is set to run the workflow (**Figure 5.137**).

4. Adjust the date, time, and repeat settings for the event within iCal. For example, set the alarm to repeat every weekday at 7:00 am (**Figure 5.138**).

There's no need to manually run the workflow. Each weekday when the iCal Alarm triggers, the workflow runs automatically, begins playing the specified iTunes playlist, and starts iTunes visuals (**Figure 5.139**).

Figure 5.139 iTunes visuals display when the workflow begins playing the specified playlist.

What you see when the workflow runs:

◆ Like the previous types of workflows, when an iCal Alarm workflow is running, the menu bar displays a ✱ icon. If the workflow runs quickly, this icon may only appear briefly, in some cases, even too briefly to see.

✔ Tip

■ For this example workflow, you won't be able to see the menu, since iTunes visuals are displayed at full screen.

To stop the running iCal Alarm workflow:

◆ While the iCal Alarm workflow is running, click the ✱ icon in the menu bar and choose Stop "iTunes Alarm Clock."

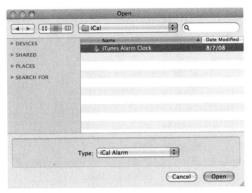

Figure 5.141 Opening an iCal Alarm workflow.

Editing an iCal Alarm workflow

Automator saves iCal Alarms workflows as specially formatted workflow applications into the ~/Library/Workflows/Applications/iCal folder on your Mac (**Figure 5.140**).

To open the workflow:

1. Within Automator, choose File > Open.

   or

   Press ⌃⌘O.

   or

   Create a new workflow window, and click the Open an Existing Workflow button in the template selection panel.

2. In the Open dialog, set the Type pop-up menu to either iCal Alarm or All.

3. Locate the desired iCal Alarm workflow and click Open (**Figure 5.141**).

   The workflow opens in Automator and is ready for editing.

✔ Tips

- When you set the Type pop-up menu in the Open dialog to iCal Alarm, Automator automatically displays the contents of the ~/Library/Workflows/Applications/iCal folder.

- To delete an iCal Alarm, first launch iCal and delete any events that are configured to run the workflow. Next, navigate to the ~/Library/Workflows/Applications/iCal folder, locate the workflow, and move it to the trash or another folder.

iCAL ALARMS

Figure 5.140 iCal Alarm workflows are saved into ~/Library/Workflows/Applications/iCal.

Image Capture Plugins

Another type of workflow that Automator supports is a plug-in for the Image Capture application, which is found in the Applications folder on your Mac. An Image Capture Plugin appears in Image Capture's interface (**Figure 5.142**). When triggered, Image Capture downloads the photos from your camera and then passes them to the workflow for further processing.

Building and saving an Image Capture Plugin workflow

Naturally, there are a lot of possibilities when it comes to Image Capture Plugins. Any workflow that manipulates images makes a good candidate—resizing, renaming, converting images from one type to another, and so on. For this example, you'll create a workflow that generates a multipage PDF of your images as you import them and attaches it to a new outgoing email message.

✔ Tip

- If you create an Image Capture Plugin that manipulates your images, be sure that it makes a copy of them first, so your originals are preserved.

Actions used:

- New PDF from Images
- New Mail Message

To build the workflow:

1. Create a new Automator workflow. When the template selection panel appears, choose to create an Image Capture Plugin, and then click Choose (**Figure 5.143**).

   A new workflow window appears, and its header area indicates that the Image Capture Plugin receives image files as input (**Figure 5.144**).

Image Capture Plugin

Figure 5.142 Image Capture Plugin workflows can be run by the Image Capture application.

Image Capture Plugin button

Figure 5.143 Creating an Image Capture Plugin workflow.

Figure 5.144 The header bar of an Image Capture Plugin workflow lets you know the workflow processes image files.

IMAGE CAPTURE PLUGINS

Figure 5.145 The New PDF from Images action merges your downloaded images together into a multipage PDF.

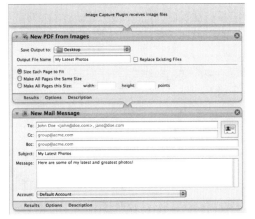

Figure 5.146 The New Mail Message action attaches the newly created PDF to an outgoing email message.

Figure 5.147 Saving an Image Capture Plugin workflow.

2. From the PDFs category, drag the New PDF from Images action to the workflow area.

3. Enter My Latest Photos in the Output File Name text field.

The action should already be set to create the PDF on the Desktop, not to overwrite existing files, and to scale each page to fit. No additional configuration is necessary (**Figure 5.145**).

4. From the Mail category, add the New Mail Message action to the end of the workflow.

If desired, enter default values into the Subject and Message fields (**Figure 5.146**).

To save the workflow:

1. Choose File > Save or press ⌃ ⌘ S.

or

To save an existing Image Capture Plugin using a new name, choose File > Save As or press ⇧Shift ⌃ ⌘ S.

Automator displays the Save panel.

2. In the "Save Image Capture Plugin as" field, type Send PDF Preview Email (**Figure 5.147**).

3. Click Save.

Automator saves the workflow as an Image Capture Plugin and installs it into the proper location on your machine.

IMAGE CAPTURE PLUGINS

Running an Image Capture Plugin workflow

A saved Image Capture Plugin automatically appears in the Image Capture application and is accessible when a camera is connected.

To run the workflow:

1. Launch Image Capture.

2. Connect your digital camera to your Mac.

   Image Capture recognizes that your camera is connected and displays download options.

3. From the Import To pop-up menu at the bottom of the Image Capture window, choose the workflow Send PDF Preview Email (**Figure 5.148**).

4. Click Import All to begin downloading the images (**Figure 5.149**).

   Image Capture downloads the images into the Pictures folder in your home folder.

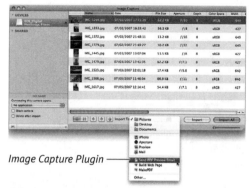

Image Capture Plugin

Figure 5.148 Selecting an Image Capture Plugin to run after your images are downloaded.

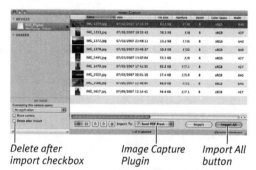

Delete after import checkbox   *Image Capture Plugin*   *Import All button*

Figure 5.149 Image Capture, ready to import images and run the workflow.

— PDF of images

Figure 5.150 A Mail message generated by the Send PDF Preview Email Image Capture Plugin.

Figure 5.151 A PDF of images generated by the Send PDF Preview Email Image Capture Plugin.

After all images have been downloaded to your Mac (to the ~/Pictures folder, by default), Image Capture passes the paths to those images to the Send PDF Preview Email workflow for processing. Next, the workflow generates a PDF of the images on the desktop and attaches it to a new Mail message (**Figures 5.150** and **5.151**).

✔ Tip

■ To ensure that your images aren't permanently deleted from the camera after import, make sure the "Delete after import" checkbox is *not* selected in Image Capture (Figure 5.149).

What you see when the workflow runs:

◆ As an Image Capture Plugin workflow runs, the menu bar displays a ✿ icon. If the workflow runs quickly, this icon may only appear briefly, in some cases, even too briefly to see.

To stop the running Image Capture Plugin workflow:

◆ While the Image Capture Plugin workflow is running, click the ✿ icon in the menu bar and choose Stop "Send PDF Preview Email."

IMAGE CAPTURE PLUGINS

Editing an Image Capture Plugin workflow

Image Capture Plugin workflows are saved as specially formatted workflow applications in the ~/Library/Workflows/Applications/ Image Capture folder on your Mac (**Figure 5.152**).

To open the workflow:

1. Within Automator, choose File > Open.

   or

   Press ⌃ ⌘ O.

   or

   Create a new workflow window, and click the Open an Existing Workflow button in the template selection panel.

2. In the Open dialog, set the Type pop-up menu to either Image Capture Plugin or All.

3. Locate the desired Image Capture Plugin and click Open (**Figure 5.153**).

   The Image Capture Plugin workflow opens in Automator and is ready for editing.

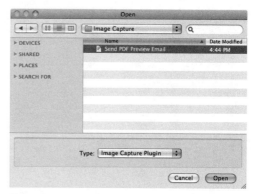

Figure 5.153 Opening an Image Capture Plugin workflow.

✔ Tips

■ When you set the Type pop-up menu in the Open dialog to Image Capture Plugin, Automator automatically displays the contents of the ~/Library/Workflows/ Applications/Image Capture folder.

■ To delete or remove an Image Capture Plugin, navigate to the ~/Library/ Workflows/Applications/Image Capture folder, locate the workflow, and move it to the trash or another folder. When you do this, the workflow no longer appears in Image Capture.

Figure 5.152 Image Capture Plugin workflows are saved into ~/Library/Workflows/Applications/Image Capture.

Figure 5.154 A workflow Application opened in Automator.

Figure 5.155 A new, empty Service workflow, configured to process image files in the Finder.

Converting Workflow Types

Odds are that at some point you'll build a workflow of a certain type and then decide you want it to be another type of workflow. For example, suppose you've created a useful workflow Application. After using it for a few weeks, you may decide that it would be much more efficient as a Service workflow, which you could run using a keyboard shortcut.

You've learned that you can toggle between a Workflow file and an Application during the save process. For other types of workflows, however, it's not quite as easy. Automator doesn't provide a quick and straightforward path for converting workflows from one type to another—at least at the time this book was written—except with Workflows and Applications.

Regardless, this is likely something you'll need to do at some point. Fortunately, there is a workaround method.

To convert a workflow from one type to another:

1. Open the existing workflow in Automator. For example, you might open a workflow Application (**Figure 5.154**).

2. Create a new workflow of the desired type, such as a Service, and configure any options in its header area, if any. For example, if your Application processed files, you might configure your Service to process image files in the Finder (**Figure 5.155**).

continues on next page

3. Select all the actions in the existing work-flow (press ⌃⌘A) and drag them to the new workflow (**Figure 5.156**).

Automator copies the actions into the new workflow, retaining their settings (**Figure 5.157**). You're now ready to final-ize and save the new workflow.

While this workaround method may work in most situations, please be aware that not everything will always come across as smoothly as you might expect. For example, disabled actions may become enabled in the new workflow. In addition, some workflow variables may not copy as expected. When converting workflows in this manner, take care. Be sure to double-check the actions and other aspects of the new workflow, and conduct thorough testing to ensure that the workflow behaves as expected.

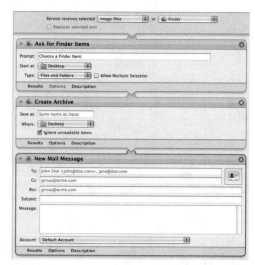

Figure 5.157 A Service workflow containing actions copied from a workflow Application.

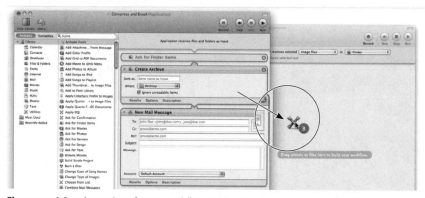

Figure 5.156 Copying actions from a workflow Application to a Service workflow.

CONVERTING WORKFLOW TYPES

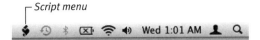

Script menu

Figure 5.158 The system-wide Script menu in Mac OS X.

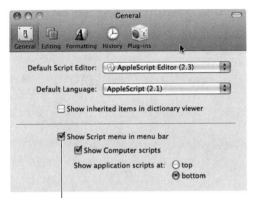

Option to show the Script
menu in the menu bar

Figure 5.159 The Script menu is enabled from AppleScript Editor's Preferences window.

Script Menu

Mac OS X has a system-wide Script menu that, when enabled, appears in the menu bar at all times (**Figure 5.158**). This Script menu provides quick access to AppleScripts, PERL scripts, Shell scripts, and Automator workflows from within any application.

In Mac OS X 10.4 Tiger and 10.5 Leopard, Automator let you save workflows as Script Menu Plugins. Although this capability no longer exists, most likely due to Automator now allowing you to save workflows into the system-wide Services menu, you may still manually add workflows to the Script menu, if desired.

By default, the Script menu is disabled.

To enable the Script menu:

1. Launch AppleScript Editor, which is found in the /Applications/Utilities folder.

2. Choose AppleScript Editor > Preferences. A Preferences window appears.

3. Click General in the Preferences window's toolbar, if it's not already selected.

4. Select the "Show Script menu in menu bar" checkbox (**Figure 5.159**).

SCRIPT MENU

To add Automator workflows to the Script menu:

1. Navigate to the ~/Library/Scripts folder. If this folder doesn't exist, you can create it manually.

   or

   Select Open Scripts Folder > Open User Scripts Folder from the Script menu (**Figure 5.160**). If the folder doesn't exist, it is created for you automatically.

2. Copy the desired Automator work-flows into the ~/Library/Scripts folder (**Figure 5.161**).

   The workflows now appear in the Script menu. You can select them to run them (**Figure 5.162**).

✔ Tip

■ To remove an Automator workflow from the Script menu, go to ~/Library/Scripts, and delete the desired workflow.

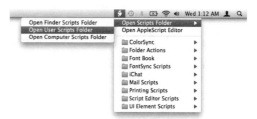

Figure 5.160 Opening the ~/Library/Scripts folder via the Script menu.

Figure 5.161 The ~/Library/Scripts folder, which includes some Automator workflows.

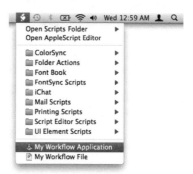

Figure 5.162 The Script menu, displaying some Automator workflows, ready to be run.

RECORDING
MANUAL EVENTS

Perhaps one of Automator's most useful features is its capability to record what you do manually and play it back as part of a workflow. When you record manual tasks, Automator watches your keystrokes, mouse movements, and clicks. Any individual task you perform with your keyboard or mouse is considered an event. When you're done, Automator saves these events in an action, allowing you to play them back later when your workflow runs.

The capability to record means that Automator can perform almost any task you can do manually on your Mac. Even if Automator actions aren't available for a particular application, you may still be able to automate them through recording. This chapter covers what you need to know about recording and playing back manual tasks within a workflow.

Enabling Recording

Before you can record manual events with Automator, you must enable Accessibility on your machine. Accessibility is a Mac OS X feature that allows applications and processes to watch your mouse clicks, text typing, and so on. Without Accessibility enabled, Automator can't watch you do things and thus can't record them in a workflow.

✔ Tip

■ Recording with Automator is not possible in Tiger (Mac OS X v10.4). It's a feature that was introduced with Leopard (Mac OS X 10.5).

To enable Accessibility:

1. From the Apple menu, choose System Preferences (**Figure 6.1**).

   The System Preferences application launches and displays the System Preferences window.

2. In the lower-right corner of Preferences, click the Universal Access icon (**Figure 6.2**).

   The system displays your current Universal Access preferences.

Figure 6.1 Opening System Preferences from the Apple menu.

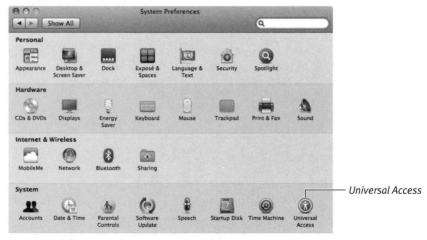

Universal Access

Figure 6.2 Locating the Universal Access system preference.

3. Select the "Enable access for assistive devices" checkbox to enable Accessibility (**Figure 6.3**).

✔ Tips

■ You need administrator access to turn on Accessibility.

■ If you forget to enable Accessibility, don't worry. If you try to start recording without it, Automator reminds you to turn it on.

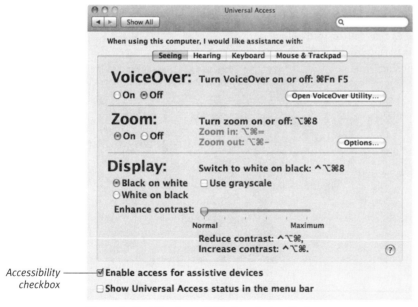

Accessibility checkbox

Figure 6.3 Enabling Accessibility from System Preferences.

ENABLING RECORDING

Recording Manual Tasks

You can record manual events in an empty Automator workflow or in a workflow that contains existing actions. There's no need to insert a new action; Automator takes care of this for you automatically when you stop recording.

To record manual events:

1. Create a new workflow or open a saved one.

2. Choose Workflow > Record (**Figure 6.4**).

   or

   Press (Option)(⌃)(⌘)(R).

   or

   Click the Record button in the Automator workflow toolbar (**Figure 6.5**).

   If you have not enabled Accessibility, you are prompted to do so now (**Figure 6.6**). To cancel recording, click the Cancel button. Or, to enable Accessibility, click the Open Universal Access button and follow the instructions in the previous section, "Enabling Recording."

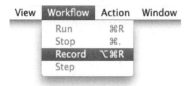

Figure 6.4 The menu method of beginning to record an Automator workflow.

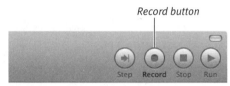

Figure 6.5 The icon method of beginning to record an Automator workflow.

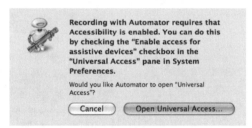

Figure 6.6 A message indicating that Accessibility is not enabled on your machine.

Preparing for Recording

Before you begin to record, think things through! Anticipate what steps you want to record, and prepare for them. For example, suppose your workflow uses the New TextEdit Document action to create a document in TextEdit. You then want the workflow to perform a series of recorded steps on that document. Before recording the steps, you'll need to replicate the environment that will be encountered at runtime. In this case, make sure that a TextEdit document exists, and then begin recording.

Figure 6.7 Automator in recording mode.

When you begin recording, Automator hides your workflow window and displays a small recording mode indicator (**Figure 6.7**). You can now bring the desired application to the front and begin your tasks. Automator watches you and keeps track of your key presses and mouse clicks.

When you've finished your manual tasks, stop recording and return to your workflow.

✔ Tips

- For you to record manual events within an application, that application must support accessibility.

- Automator may not record absolutely everything you do. You may encounter certain tasks that are simply not recordable.

- Automator may sometimes record events that you don't want or need in your workflow. If this happens, you can remove any unwanted events when you're done recording.

- When recording, go slowly. It may take Automator a second or two to recognize what you've clicked or typed. Giving Automator time to keep up is always a good idea.

Know When to Record

Look for existing actions first. Before recording a manual task, see if an Automator action exists for that task. If it does, use it. It will probably run faster in your workflow, work more reliably, and give you more control over the task being performed.

To stop recording:

1. Select the Automator recording window.

2. Click the Stop button in the Automator recording window (**Figure 6.8**).

   or

   Press ⌃ ⌘ . .

   or

   Bring Automator to the front by clicking its icon in the Dock. Then choose Workflow > Stop (**Figure 6.9**).

   Automator closes the recording window, and your workflow becomes visible, prefilled with a new Watch Me Do action at the end of the workflow. This action includes a list of all the manual events that were recorded. You can view additional information about an event, such as the application it targets, by clicking it (**Figure 6.10**).

Stop button —

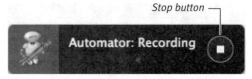

Figure 6.8 The icon method of stopping Automator from recording.

Figure 6.9 The menu method of stopping Automator from recording.

Recorded manual tasks —   ┌ Event details

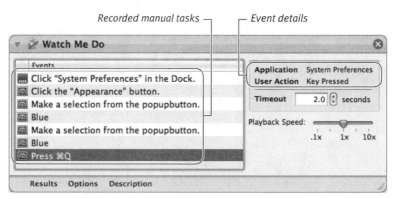

Figure 6.10 Viewing the details of a recorded event.

RECORDING MANUAL TASKS

✔ Tips

- After you stop recording, if you realize that you need to record more, don't panic. Simply begin recording again. Automator will record the additional events and insert a second Watch Me Do action into your workflow.

- Recording may not always work as anticipated. When you're finished recording, it's always a good idea to play the recorded events. If they don't do exactly what you expect, try recording them again. If they still don't work, try doing them in a different way. For example, if creating a new document in an application is giving you trouble, instead of choosing File > New, try pressing ⌃ ⌘ N.

- In some cases, you may need to try recording a set of manual tasks several times for Automator to get them right. Just be sure to take it slow.

- Some applications need to be in the front for Automator to interact with them. If your recorded steps don't bring an application to the front, try inserting the Launch Application action, found in the Utilities category, before the Watch Me Do action and telling it to launch the desired application.

Third-party Macro Utilities

Aside from Automator, there are some useful third-party macro utilities available for Mac OS X. QuicKeys (www.quickeys. com) and iKey (www.scriptsoftware.com/ ikey) are two popular commercial utilities that can perform mouse clicks and keystrokes. In some cases, these applications may even be able to perform tasks that Automator can't. If you get into a bind recording in Automator, try one of these great tools. QuicKeys even includes an Automator action that allows you to trigger a macro from within an Automator workflow.

Removing Recorded Events

When recording manual tasks, keep in mind that Automator records what you do. This may not, however, always be what you want the workflow to do when run. Sometimes extra steps are recorded, or you may decide that a step is no longer necessary. In these cases, you can delete individual recorded events, leaving only the ones you need.

To remove a recorded event:

1. Select the events that you want to delete in the list of events on the left side of the Watch Me Do action (**Figure 6.11**).

2. Press (Delete).

   Automator removes the selected events from the action (**Figure 6.12**).

✔ Tip

■ Once you remove an event from the Watch Me Do action, there's no way to get it back. So, before deleting an event, make sure you really want to delete it.

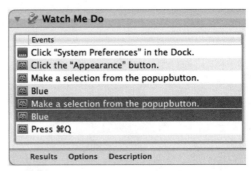

Figure 6.11 Selecting recorded events in the Watch Me Do action.

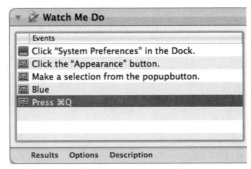

Figure 6.12 The Watch Me Do action after deleting some events.

Preparing to Play Recorded Events

Recorded events are played when your workflow is run. Before this, however, you may want to make some adjustments to their behavior.

Event playback timeouts

When an individual event plays, Automator gives it a limited amount of time to finish; this is called a *timeout*. For example, you wouldn't want Automator to try selecting a checkbox in a window before that window has fully opened. By default, timeouts are two seconds. In rare circumstances, however, this may not be enough. The Watch Me Do action allows you to adjust the timeouts for individual events, if needed.

To increase an event's playback timeout:

1. In your workflow, select the desired event within the Watch Me Do action.

2. In the Timeout field, enter the maximum number of seconds you'd like Automator to allow for the event to complete (**Figure 6.13**).

   When your workflow is run, Automator will then allow the specified number of seconds for the event to execute.

Selected event   Playback Timeout

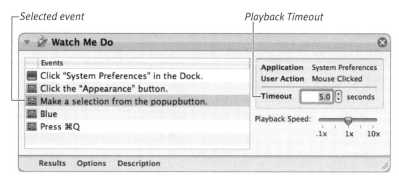

Figure 6.13 Adjusting the playback timeout for a recorded event.

Playback speed

By default, Automator plays back recorded events at the speed you recorded them. When you need to get a job done quicker, you can increase the playback speed of the Watch Me Do action. This affects the speed of the events as a whole, not the speed of an individual event. You can also play events more slowly should the rare need arise.

To adjust the playback speed of recorded events:

Set the Playback Speed slider in the Watch Me Do action within your workflow to the desired speed. To decrease playback speed, move the slider to the left. To increase playback speed, move the slider to the right (**Figure 6.14**).

✔ Tip

■ Don't move a muscle. When playing recorded tasks, avoid moving the mouse or pressing keys. Doing so can interfere with the events being played, and in some cases, may cause them to produce an error.

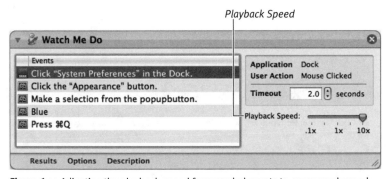

Figure 6.14 Adjusting the playback speed for recorded events to 10x normal speed.

WORKFLOW LOOPING

Until now, all of the Automator workflows you've created run in sequence from the first action in the workflow to the last—and then they're done. One time through, and that's it. In most cases, this type of workflow execution works just fine. In some cases, however, you may need something a bit more robust: a looping workflow that repeats a series of tasks over and over.

For example, suppose you want a workflow that takes a series of time-delayed screen shots for troubleshooting purposes, and then emails them to you for viewing on your iPhone. Sure, you could create this workflow without looping, but it would involve using the same actions over and over again and it would not continue running indefinitely.

In cases like this, it's generally much simpler to create a looping workflow that runs the same actions continually. This helps to keep your workflow manageable while providing the repeating functionality you need.

About Looping

One way to create a looping workflow is to save the workflow as an iCal Alarm plug-in and set it to run on a repeating schedule (see "iCal Alarms" in Chapter 5, "Types of Workflows"). For simple workflows, however, this technique may be overkill, or it may not meet your specific needs. For example, you may want to run the workflow from the Script menu or Image Capture, not from iCal. Or, you may want the workflow to loop only until you tell it to stop, to loop for a specific amount of time, and so forth.

In these situations, Automator's Loop action (located in the Utilities category) may be what you need. You can insert this action anywhere in your workflow to create a repeating workflow (**Figure 7.1**). When encountered at runtime, the Loop action causes your workflow to go back to the first action and start over again. This action has two main options—looping method and input handling.

Figure 7.1 Use the Loop action to create a repeating workflow.

Sorry Tiger Users

The Loop action wasn't released until Leopard (Mac OS X 10.5). It is, however, still possible to create a looping workflow in Tiger (Mac OS X 10.4). Here are some options:

◆ **Run Workflow.** Consider inserting this action, located in the Automator category in Tiger, at the end of your workflow. Configure it to run your workflow again, thus creating a never-ending loop.

◆ **Automator Loop Utility.** Google this little gem, and you should find an AppleScript-based application that you can use to create looping workflow applications.

◆ **iCal Alarm Plug-in.** Consider saving your workflow as an iCal Alarm Plug-in and configuring it to run on a repeating schedule. In many cases, this may work just fine.

Figure 7.2 The Loop action can be set to ask you to continue before starting a loop or to loop automatically.

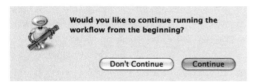

Figure 7.3 If the Loop action is set to ask to continue, Automator displays an alert when the workflow runs.

Figure 7.4 When looping automatically, you can choose to loop a specified number of times or for a specified number of minutes.

Looping method

The Loop action's first pop-up menu allows you to specify the looping method: whether the workflow should ask to continue looping or loop automatically (**Figure 7.2**). It contains two choices:

◆ **Ask to continue.** Instructs the Loop action to display an alert asking if you'd like to continue looping. You can choose to continue looping or stop looping and run any remaining actions in the workflow (**Figure 7.3**).

When you choose this option, the action disables the "Stop after" field and pop-up menu in the Loop action.

◆ **Loop automatically.** Instructs the Loop action to loop a specified number of times or for a specified period of time.

When you select this option, the action enables the "Stop after" text field and pop-up menu. You can now specify whether the workflow should stop after a certain number of times or a certain number of minutes (**Figure 7.4**).

✔ Tips

■ Unfortunately, the Loop action doesn't include an option to loop indefinitely. To do this, one option is to set the workflow to loop a high number of times. You can set the Loop action to loop up to 1000 times. Another option is to add the Run Workflow action, found in the Utilities category, to the end of your workflow and set it to run your workflow again.

■ Need a break? Insert the Pause action, found in the Utilities category, to make your workflow delay for a specified amount of time between loops.

ABOUT LOOPING

Input handling

The Loop action's second pop-up menu lets you specify whether the original input or current results should be used in each loop (**Figure 7.5**). It contains two choices:

◆ **Use the original input.** Instructs the Loop action to pass the workflow's original input back to the first action to be processed again.

◆ **Use the current results as input.** Instructs the Loop action to pass the results of the previous action to the first action in the workflow.

✔ Tips

■ If you add actions to your workflow after a Loop action, those actions run after Automator exits the loop.

■ When a loop exits, anything received as input by the Loop action is passed to the next action in the workflow for further processing.

Figure 7.5 Setting the Loop action to use the original input rather than the current results as input during each loop.

ABOUT LOOPING

Basic Looping Workflows

Most of the looping workflows you create are likely to be normal Automator workflows that are simply configured to run a specified number of times, for a specified amount of time, or until you tell the workflow to stop looping. Typically, these workflows start fresh with each new loop, processing their original input time and time again.

Building and running a basic looping workflow

Applications such as iChat and iMovie allow you to put your Mac's built-in iSight camera to good use—video chatting with friends, recording short movies, and more. There are lots of possibilities, and Automator gives you even more.

In the "Processing Photos and Images" section of Bonus Chapter 13, "Workflow Starting Points," available online (see Introduction), you learned how to use Automator to take photos when your workflow runs. You'll put that technique to good use in this example.

Here, you'll create a looping workflow that takes a series of delayed photos and stitches them together into a QuickTime time-lapse movie. With this workflow, you'll finally be able to see what your cat really does while you're at work, make sure the kids are doing their homework after school, or watch the leaves fall outside your window.

✔ Tip

■ To run this workflow, you must have QuickTime 7 installed. This is an optional install on the Snow Leopard installation disk. Once installed, QuickTime 7 is found in your /Applications/Utilities folder.

Looping Through Files

Unfortunately, Automator's Loop action does not allow you to individually process files through a workflow. If you pass 700 files to the first action in the workflow, all 700 of those files are passed through the workflow as a group. Depending on the workflow, this may be problematic.

For example, suppose your workflow consists of four actions that perform four separate tasks: open a file, modify the file, save the file, and close the file. If you send 700 files through the workflow for processing, the first action opens all 700 files, then the workflow modifies all 700 files, saves all 700, and closes all 700.

Naturally, it's not practical to process files in this manner. For starters, most applications would not even allow you to open 700 files at one time. As a workaround, I have developed a freeware AppleScript application that you can use to individually send dropped files to an Automator workflow application. You can download the Automator Multi-Item Processing Utility from www.automatedworkflows. com/software/automator_actions/ automator_tools.html.

Another third-party solution to this problem is the Dispense Items Incrementally action. This action works in combination with Automator's Loop action. Simply add the action to a workflow and pass it some files and folders as input. During each loop, it releases one file or folder at a time for processing. You can download the Dispense Items Incrementally action from www.macosxautomation.com/ automator/examples/actions.html.

Actions used:

- ◆ Take Video Snapshot
- ◆ Pause
- ◆ Loop
- ◆ Get Specified Finder Items
- ◆ Get Folder Contents
- ◆ Rename Finder Items
- ◆ New QuickTime Slideshow

To build the workflow:

1. Create a new folder on the desktop and name it Snapshots (**Figure 7.6**).

2. Bring Automator to the front and create a new Workflow file.

3. From the Photos category, drag the Take Video Snapshot action to the workflow area.

   From the Where pop-up in the action's interface, select Other. Locate the Snapshots folder you created on the desktop. Then select the "Take picture automatically" checkbox. You can leave the Save as field set to its default value (**Figure 7.7**).

4. From the Utilities category, drag the Pause action to the workflow area.

   Type 1 into the action's field, and set the following pop-up to "minutes."

   This instructs the workflow to delay for one minute after each snapshot has been taken (**Figure 7.8**).

Figure 7.6 The Snapshots folder is accessed when your workflow runs.

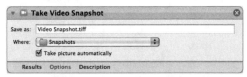

Figure 7.7 The Take Video Snapshot action takes a photo using your Mac's built-in camera.

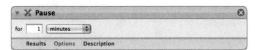

Figure 7.8 Use the Pause action to delay a workflow for a specified amount of time.

Figure 7.9 The Loop action causes the workflow to run over and over again.

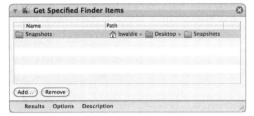

Figure 7.10 The Get Specified Finder Items action locates the Snapshots folder after the loop exits.

Figure 7.11 The Get Folder Contents action retrieves photos from the Snapshots folder.

5. From the Utilities category, drag the Loop action to the workflow area.

From the first pop-up menu in the Loop action, choose "Loop automatically." Set the "Stop after" field to 120, and ensure that its pop-up menu is set to "minutes." Choose "Use the original input" from the second pop-up menu (**Figure 7.9**).

6. From the Files & Folders category, drag the Get Specified Finder Items action to the workflow area.

Click Add and choose the Snapshots folder (**Figure 7.10**).

7. With the Get Specified Finder Items action selected in the workflow area, choose Ignore Input from the Action menu.

This is done so that the action doesn't append the Loop action's result to the Snapshots folder that is passed to the next action for processing.

8. Drag the Get Folder Contents action from the Library list to the end of the workflow.

You can leave the "Repeat for each subfolder found" checkbox deselected (**Figure 7.11**).

This action retrieves a list of photos in the Snapshots folder when the workflow runs.

continues on next page

9. Add the Rename Finder Items action to the workflow.

Automator displays a warning indicating that this action changes the names of items passed to it. Click Don't Add to continue placing the action without inserting an additional Copy Finder Items action (**Figure 7.12**).

The action is added to the workflow, and its default title changes to Add Date or Time to Finder Item Names to reflect its current state.

From the pop-up menu at the top of the action, choose Make Sequential. The name of the action again changes to reflect its state—Make Finder Item Names Sequential. Click the "new name" radio button, and enter the name Image. You can leave all other settings set to their default values (**Figure 7.13**).

This action renames the images sequentially, so they can be merged together by QuickTime Player.

10. Select the Photos category in Automator's Actions library, and add the New QuickTime Slideshow action to the workflow.

Enter Time Lapse Movie into the Save As field. Next, set the Slide Duration pop-up to 1 seconds per image and the Default Playback pop-up to Movie, and deselect the Loop checkbox. You can leave the Format pop-up to Self-contained and the output folder set to the Desktop (**Figure 7.14**).

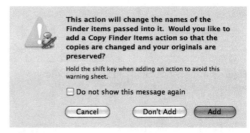

Figure 7.12 Automator warns you that the Rename Finder Items action modifies the names of your files.

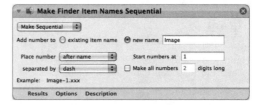

Figure 7.13 Rename Finder Items makes your images sequential, so they can be stitched together by QuickTime.

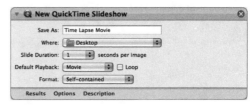

Figure 7.14 The New QuickTime Slideshow action creates a slide show movie from images it receives as input.

BASIC LOOPING WORKFLOWS

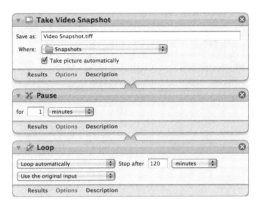

Figure 7.15 The first part of the workflow takes a snapshot, delays, and then loops.

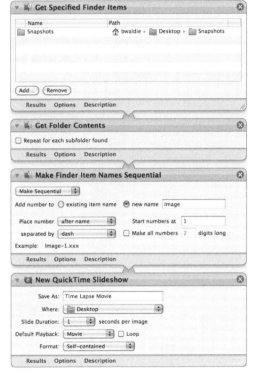

Figure 7.16 The second part of the workflow locates the snapshot images, renames them sequentially, and then merges them into a time-lapse movie.

The workflow is now complete and is ready to be run (**Figures 7.15** and **7.16**).

✔ Tips

■ During testing, you may not want the workflow to delay for one minute in between loops or to wait 120 minutes before exiting the loop. Feel free to adjust these settings as needed. For example, you can set the workflow to pause for ten seconds and exit the repeat after one minute.

■ A faster way to insert and configure the Get Specified Finder Items action is to simply drag the Snapshots folder from your desktop directly into your Automator workflow.

To run the workflow:

1. Launch QuickTime Player 7.

2. Click the Run button in Automator's tool-bar, or press ⌃⌘R to run the workflow.

   The workflow begins running.

   A video snapshot is taken first and saved to the Snapshots folder on the desktop. The workflow pauses for one minute, and then loops back to the beginning.

   The workflow proceeds in this manner for 120 minutes, at which point it exits the loop and continues with the remainder of the workflow.

   The workflow locates the Snapshots folder, retrieves a list of images in that folder, renames them, and merges them together in a QuickTime movie slide show, which is saved to the desktop (**Figure 7.17**).

Figure 7.17 The result of the workflow is a time-lapse QuickTime movie of snapshot photos.

✔ Tips

- To build a series of time-lapse movies, try creating this workflow as an iCal Alarm rather than a Workflow file. Then set it to run every day.

- Going on a vacation? You could configure this workflow to email you time-lapse movies, so you can check in on your home or office while you're away.

- To clean up the images after they've been merged together as a QuickTime slide show movie, use another Get Specified Finder Items action (set to ignore its input) to get the Snapshots folder again. Then use the Move Finder Items action to move the snapshot images to the trash.

Advanced Looping Workflows

Automator's Loop action also enables you to create a more advanced type of looping workflow—one that passes the last looped action's result as input to the first action in the workflow. For example, you might need to create a workflow application that accepts a dropped folder as input, renames the folder, gets a list of subfolders within the folder, and then performs the same process again on those subfolders. Workflows of this nature are likely to be pretty rare, but Automator is ready to help if you need to create one.

Building and running an advanced looping workflow

For this example, you'll create a workflow application that accepts a dropped image file as input. Once triggered, the workflow copies the image to the desktop, scales it to 50 percent of its original size, and renames it to Scaled Image.

The workflow then loops, passing the resulting Scaled Image file back to the beginning of the workflow. Again, Automator copies the image to the desktop, scales it to 50 percent of its already diminished size, and renames it Scaled Image 2.

The result is two images on the desktop: Scaled Image, which is 50 percent the size of the original dropped image, and Scaled Image 2, which is 50 percent the size of Scaled Image. A workflow of this nature might come in handy when preparing images for inclusion on a website.

Actions used:

- ◆ Copy Finder Items
- ◆ Scale Images
- ◆ Rename Finder Items
- ◆ Loop

To build the workflow:

1. Create a new workflow Application.

2. From the Files & Folders category, drag the Copy Finder Items action to the workflow area.

   This action should be configured to copy items to the Desktop by default. No further adjustments are necessary (**Figure 7.18**).

3. From the Photos category, drag the Scale Images action to the workflow area.

   Choose By Percentage from the Scale Images action's pop-up menu. Enter 50 into the Scale Images action's field (**Figure 7.19**).

4. From the Files & Folders category, drag the Rename Finder Items action to the workflow area.

5. Automator displays an alert suggesting that you insert a Copy Finder Items action first to preserve the names of your original images.

   Because the first action in the workflow is already Copy Finder Items, this is unnecessary. Click Don't Add.

   Automator adds the Rename Finder Items action to the workflow, displaying the default title Add Date or Time to Finder Item Names.

Figure 7.18 The Copy Finder Items action copies items passed to the workflow to the Desktop.

Figure 7.19 Set the Scale Images action to resize images to 50 percent.

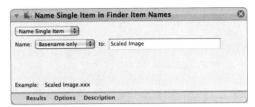

Figure 7.20 Configuring the Rename Finder Items action.

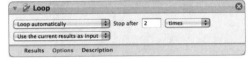

Figure 7.21 Configuring the Loop action to loop automatically twice and to use the current results as input.

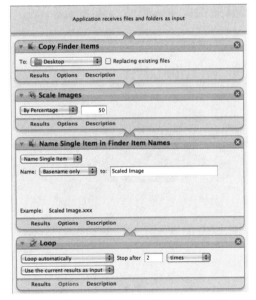

Figure 7.22 The completed workflow consists of four actions: Copy Finder Items, Scale Images, Rename Finder Items, and Loop.

6. Choose Name Single Item from the first pop-up menu in the Rename Finder Items action.

   The action's title changes to Name Single Item in Finder Item Names, and its interface changes to display some new options.

7. Choose "Basename only" from the Name pop-up menu, and enter a value of Scaled Image into the "to" text field (**Figure 7.20**).

8. From the Utilities category, drag the Loop action to the workflow area.

9. Choose "Loop automatically" from the first pop-up menu in the Loop action.

   Automator enables the "Stop after" field and pop-up menu.

10. Type 2 into the "Stop after" field, and choose "times" from the "Stop after" pop-up menu.

11. Choose "Use the current results as input" from the second pop-up menu (**Figure 7.21**).

    Your workflow is now complete and ready to be saved. It consists of four actions: Copy Finder Items, Scale Images, Rename Finder Items, and Loop (**Figure 7.22**).

✔ Tip

■ A basename is the name of a file minus its extension.

To save the workflow:

1. Choose File > Save (or press ⌃ ⌘ S).
   The save panel appears.

2. Type Scale Image to 50-50 into the Save As text field.

3. Choose Desktop from the Where pop-up menu.

4. Choose Application from the File Format pop-up menu.

5. Click Save (**Figure 7.23**).
   Automator saves the workflow as an application named Scale Image to 50-50 on your desktop. It's now ready to run.

To run the workflow:

◆ Locate an image file and drag it onto the Scale Image to 50-50 workflow application on your desktop.
   The workflow begins running.

As the workflow runs, it copies the dropped image file to the desktop, scales it to 50 percent, and renames it as Scaled Image.

The Loop action then runs the workflow a second time. This time the first action receives the newly scaled image file as input, copies it to the desktop, and resizes it to 50 percent. Because there's already a file on the desktop named Scaled Image, the Rename Finder Items action names the new image Scaled Image 2.

You now have two scaled images on your desktop. The first, Scaled Image, is resized to 50 percent of the original dropped image. The second, Scaled Image 2, is resized to 50 percent of the first scaled image (**Figures 7.24, 7.25,** and **7.26**).

Figure 7.23 Save the workflow to your desktop as an application named Scale Image to 50-50.

Figure 7.24 The originally dropped image is at its full size.

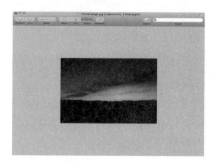

Figure 7.25 The first resized image, named Scaled Image, is 50 percent of the original.

Figure 7.26 The second resized image, named Scaled Image 2, is 50 percent of the first resized image.

ADVANCED LOOPING WORKFLOWS

USING VARIABLES

The way information passes through an Automator workflow is fairly simple: It passes in sequence from action to action. Sometimes, however, problems arise—actions don't produce a result, or actions need information from an action much earlier in the workflow. Although such scenarios are less likely to occur in simple workflows, they can severely limit your ability to create complex workflows. Automator's workflow variables can help tremendously.

Variables allow you to store information (such as an action's result) at one point in a workflow and then refer back to it at a later point. They also allow you to retrieve dynamic content (such as the current date or time, or the current user's name) and use it when your workflow runs. In essence, a variable is nothing more than stored information; it can be a reference to a file or folder, some text, or almost anything else.

In this chapter, you'll learn how to incorporate variables into your workflows, including storing and retrieving action results, using variables to reference dynamic content, and more. You'll also create some example workflows that incorporate variables, including one that downloads images from a Safari webpage into a dated folder on your desktop.

Types of Variables

Like actions, variables are organized into categories within Automator's Library list (**Figure 8.1**). The available categories of variables are:

◆ **Date & Time (Figure 8.2).** These variables enable your workflow to retrieve and use information such as the current day, current month, and current time. For example, you could use a Date & Time variable to append the current time to the name of a file created by your workflow.

◆ **Locations (Figure 8.3).** These variables enable your workflow to easily reference folders on your Mac, such as when saving a file, backing up files and folders, and more. Predefined variables exist for commonly accessed folders, including Applications, Documents, and Favorites. The category's *Path* variable also enables you to create a custom location mapped to the folder of your choice.

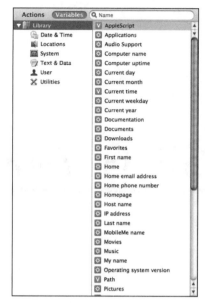

Figure 8.1 Displayed in Automator's Library list, variables are organized into categories by type.

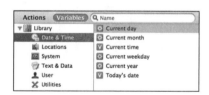

Figure 8.2 Automator's Date & Time category of variables.

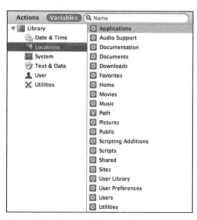

Figure 8.3 Automator's Locations category of variables.

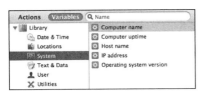

Figure 8.4 Automator's System category of variables.

Figure 8.5 Automator's Text & Data category of variables.

Figure 8.6 Automator's User category of variables.

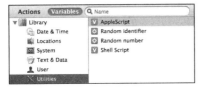

Figure 8.7 Automator's Utilities category of variables.

◆ **System (Figure 8.4).** These variables enable your workflow to retrieve information about the current system configuration, including IP address, operating system version, and the amount of time the computer has been running. These variables could be useful in a workflow that emails troubleshooting information or status updates to a system administrator.

◆ **Text & Data (Figure 8.5).** These variables enable your workflow to store and retrieve text values, as well as other types of data, such as file and folder paths, iPhoto items, and Mail messages. Generally, the variables in this category are likely to be used mostly for storing and retrieving action results.

◆ **User (Figure 8.6).** These variables enable your workflow to retrieve information about the current user, such as the first name, last name, full name, or homepage. This information could be appended to an email message, added to a TextEdit document, and so forth.

◆ **Utilities (Figure 8.7).** These variables enable your workflow to retrieve random numbers and text, which you can use, for example, to ensure that filenames do not conflict with one another. Also included in this category are AppleScript and UNIX variables, which can be used to execute code and produce some type of dynamic value at various points within a workflow. These particular variables are fairly advanced and are probably likely to be used only by advanced Automator users.

✔ Tip

■ For an introductory overview of variables, see "About Variables" in Chapter 1, "Getting Started."

Help for Tiger Users

Workflow variables were introduced in Leopard (Mac OS X 10.5). In Tiger (Mac OS X 10.4), however, you can still store and retrieve information through the use of third-party actions. To find these actions, use Google to search for "Temporary Storage Actions for Automator."

TYPES OF VARIABLES

Adding Variables to Workflows

Automator includes dozens of variables. To use one, you must first add it to your workflow, like an action. Unlike an action, however, a variable doesn't immediately appear as part of the workflow. Rather, a variable initially appears in the workflow variables area. You can then insert the variable into different parts of your workflow whenever you want to retrieve its value. You'll learn how to retrieve the value of a variable shortly.

To add a variable to your workflow:

1. At the top of the Library list within a workflow window, click the Variables button.

   The list of categories and variables appears (**Figure 8.8**).

2. Find the variable you want to add to your workflow, such as *My name* in the User category.

   You locate a variable in the same way you locate an action—by clicking through the categories or entering a keyword into the Library list's search field (**Figure 8.9**).

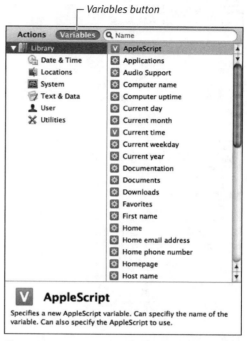

Variables button

Figure 8.8 To display a list of categories and variables, click Variables at the top of the Library list.

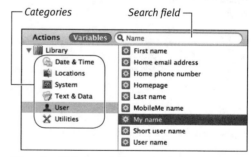

Categories   Search field

Figure 8.9 Click through the categories or enter a search term to find a variable to meet your needs.

3. Double-click the desired variable.

The workflow variables area, containing the variable, displays at the bottom of the workflow window (**Figure 8.10**).

✔ Tips

- A variable has no value when initially added to a workflow. It gets its value when you run the workflow. For example, the *My name* variable gets the name of the current user when the workflow runs.

- You can also drag variables from the Library list and drop them into the workflow variables area.

- Remember, you can learn about a variable by selecting it in the Library list and viewing its description.

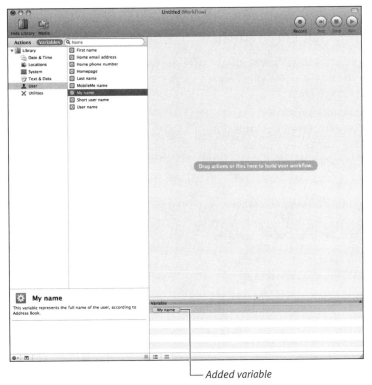

— *Added variable*

Figure 8.10 Double-click a variable in the Library list to add it to the Workflow Variables area of your workflow window.

Using Variables as Action Input

Once a variable has been added to your workflow, its value can be passed as input to an action. To do this, you use the Get Value of Variable action, which is found in the Utilities category of actions. This action retrieves the value of the specified variable, and then passes it as input to the next action in the workflow.

For example, you could create a workflow that uses a variable to retrieve the current user's name and passes it to an action that inserts that name into a new TextEdit document or Mail message.

✔ Tip

- The Get Value of Variable action is also used to retrieve stored action results.

To pass a variable value to an action:

1. From the workflow variables area, drag the variable you want to the desired location within your workflow.

   Automator automatically inserts a Get Value of Variable action at that location. The action's Variable pop-up menu is set to the specified variable.

   or

1. From the Utilities category of actions, drag the Get Value of Variable action to the desired location in the workflow area.

2. From the Variable pop-up menu, choose the desired variable (**Figure 8.11**).

When you run the workflow, the Get Value of Variable action retrieves the value of the specified variable. That value is now reflected in the result area of the Get Value of Variable action (**Figure 8.12**).

— Variable pop-up menu

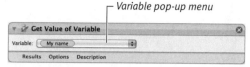

Figure 8.11 The Get Value of Variable action retrieves the value of the specified variable and passes it to the next action in the workflow.

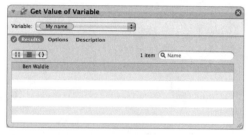

Figure 8.12 When a workflow runs, the result area of the Get Value of Variable action displays the current value of the variable.

USING VARIABLES AS ACTION INPUT

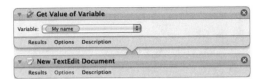

Figure 8.13 In this example, the Get Value of Variable action retrieves the value of the *My name* variable and passes it to the New TextEdit Document action for processing.

Figure 8.14 The New TextEdit Document action creates a new document in TextEdit and inserts the variable value passed as input, in this case, the name of the current user.

The variable's value is then passed as input to the next action in the workflow for processing. In this example, the Get Value of Variable action retrieves the value of the *My name* variable and passes it to the New TextEdit Document action. This action then creates a new TextEdit document containing your name (**Figures 8.13** and **8.14**).

✔ Tips

- When passing a variable to an action as input, be sure that the value of the variable matches the type of input the action accepts. Otherwise, you may get an error when you run your workflow.

- Remember, Automator doesn't know the name of the current user when the workflow is built. This value is determined when the workflow runs. Therefore, the result is different for every user.

Inserting Variables in Action Fields

Variables don't just have to be passed as input to actions. They can also be inserted into text fields and path pop-up menus within actions. This gives you a lot more flexibility when creating workflows, and it can allow for some interesting possibilities.

As an example, you could insert the *My name* variable in the Create Archive action's "Save as" text field. Now when the action runs, it automatically appends your name to the name of the archive. You could also insert a Locations variable, such as a variable pointing to the current Mac's Shared folder, to the action's Where pop-up menu (**Figure 8.15**).

✔ Tip

- Not every text field accepts variables. It's up to the action's developer to add this capability. If you drag a variable to a text field that doesn't accept variables, the variable simply is not added to the field.

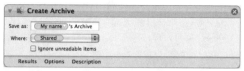

Figure 8.15 You can insert variables into text fields and path pop-up menus, allowing actions to use dynamic content in their settings. This example uses the *My name* variable to add the current user's name to the newly created archive's name. It also uses the Shared Locations variable to create the archive in the current user's Shared folder.

What's a Path Pop-up Menu?

Many Automator actions include pop-up menus that allow you to choose a file or folder. For example, an action that saves a file may let you choose an output folder. Typically, these types of pop-up menus include a list of default files or folders, such as the Desktop, your Documents folder, and so on. Often, these menus also include an Other option, allowing you to choose a custom file or folder (**Figure 8.16**).

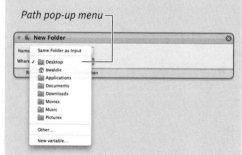

Figure 8.16 The New Folder action contains a path pop-up menu, allowing you to choose an output location for the folder.

Figure 8.17 Here, the *My name* variable is added along with some specified text to the Subject field of the New Mail Message action.

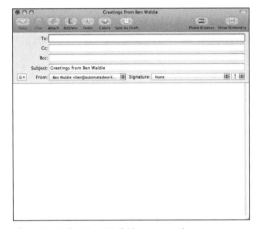

Figure 8.18 The New Mail Message action creates a new email message and inserts the value of the *My name* variable along with specified text into the Subject field.

To insert a variable in an action field:

1. Drag the variable you want from the workflow variables area to the text field or path pop-up menu in the action's interface.

or

Drag the desired variable from the Library list to the text field or path pop-up menu in the action's interface. When you do this, the variable also appears in the workflow variables area.

2. If you added the variable to a text field, you can insert additional text around the variable, if desired.

For this example, the *My name* variable is added along with some additional text to the Subject field of the New Mail Message action (**Figure 8.17**).

When the action runs within the workflow, the value of the variable is retrieved first, and then the action uses that value. In this example, your name is appended to the specified subject of the newly created Mail message (**Figure 8.18**).

To view a variable's value in an action field:

◆ For variables in text fields, click the small disclosure triangle to the right of the variable (**Figure 8.19**).

 or

 For variables in path pop-up menus, click the path pop-up menu, and then select the variable (**Figure 8.20**).

 The value of the variable is displayed. In this example, the Create Archive action creates a zip file of a folder it receives as input. The archive is named using a variable name and is created in a folder specified using a variable (**Figure 8.21**).

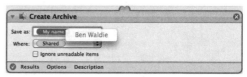

Figure 8.19 After running a workflow, click the disclosure triangle next to a text field variable to view its description.

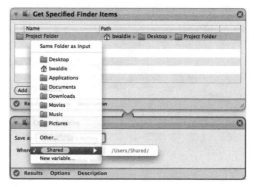

Figure 8.20 After running a workflow, select a variable in a path pop-up menu to view its description.

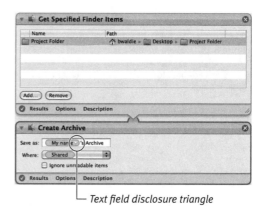

— *Text field disclosure triangle*

Figure 8.21 This workflow uses variables for the name and location when creating an archive.

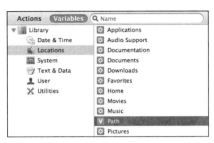

Figure 8.22 Found in the Locations category, the *Path* variable can be used to store files and folder output from an action.

Figure 8.23 Found in the Text & Data category, the *Storage* variable can be used to store any action result, whereas the new *Text* variable stores text from an action.

Result type

Figure 8.24 Check an action's description to find out its result type.

Figure 8.25 Add a variable, such as *Path*, to your workflow for the result you want to store.

Storing and Retrieving Action Results

Variables are powerful because they enable you to store an action's result and use it later in the workflow.

Depending on the type of result being stored, you use one of the following variables:

◆ *Path.* Found in the Locations category, this variable stores a reference to a file or folder output by an action (**Figure 8.22**).

◆ *Storage.* Found in the Text & Data category, this variable stores the result of an action regardless of its type. For example, it could be used to store references to iPhoto items, Mail messages, iCal events, multiple file or folder paths, and so forth (**Figure 8.23**).

◆ *Text.* This variable, also located in the Text & Data category, stores text output from an action (Figure 8.23).

To store an action's result:

1. Determine the type of action result you want to store, such as text, files and folders, Mail messages, and so forth.

   To determine the type of result for an action, look at the action's description area (**Figure 8.24**).

2. Add a variable to your workflow for the result type you would like to store.

   For example, if the action's result is files and folders, add a *Path* variable to your workflow (**Figure 8.25**).

continues on next page

3. From the Utilities category of actions, drag Set Value of Variable after the action whose result you want to store.

4. From the Variable pop-up menu, choose the variable you added to the workflow, in this case *Path* (**Figure 8.26**).

When the workflow runs, the result of the action is passed to the Set Value of Variable action, which stores it in the specified variable. In this example, the *Path* variable stores the New Folder action's result—the path to the newly created folder.

✔ Tip

■ You can create a new *Storage* variable by choosing New variable from the Set Value of Variable action's Variable pop-up menu (**Figure 8.27**).

To retrieve a stored action result:

1. Drag the variable to the desired location within the workflow.

A Get Value of Variable action is inserted for you.

2. Choose the variable from the Variable pop-up menu (**Figure 8.28**).

When you run the workflow, the Get Value of Variable action retrieves the value of the variable. The workflow variables area shows the variable's value and passes it to the next action for processing.

or

Drag the variable to a text field or pop-up menu within an action's interface (**Figure 8.29**).

When you run the workflow, Automator retrieves the variable's value and uses it in the action's setting.

In this example, the *Path* variable stores the result of the New Folder action, the newly created folder. This variable is then

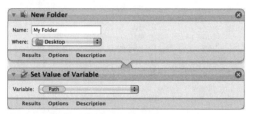

Figure 8.26 The Set Value of Variable sets a variable's value to the preceding action's result. In this example, the New Folder action's result is the path to the newly created folder, which is then stored in the *Path* variable.

Figure 8.27 Create a *Storage* variable by choosing New variable from the Set Value of Variable action's Variable pop-up menu.

Figure 8.28 Use the Get Value of Variable action to retrieve an action result stored in a variable and pass it to an action for processing.

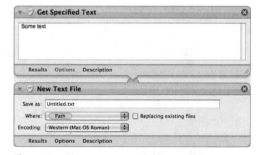

Figure 8.29 You can use a variable containing a stored action result in action text fields and pop-up menus.

referenced in the Where field of the New Text File action. When the workflow runs, Automator first creates a folder named My Folder on the desktop. Next, it creates a text file within that folder (**Figure 8.30**).

To verify the value of the *Path* variable after the workflow runs, select the variable's name in the New Text File action's Where pop-up menu (**Figure 8.31**).

Figure 8.30 In this example, the result of the New Folder action is stored in the *Path* variable. It's then later referenced in the Where pop-up menu of the New Text File action.

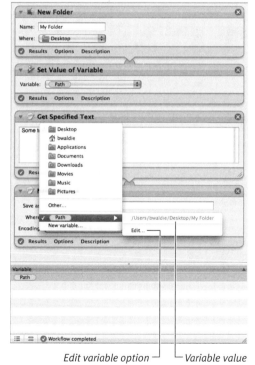

Edit variable option ⌐ ⌐ Variable value

Figure 8.31 After the workflow runs, the New Text File's path pop-up menu shows that the *New Path* variable contains the path to the newly created folder.

Adjusting Variable Options

Some Automator variables are customizable, allowing you to change the variable's name or behavior when run within a workflow. *Current time* is one such variable. When you add it to a workflow, you may want to specify the format in which the time is retrieved. For example, in some instances, you may want hours and minutes; in others, you may want hours, minutes, and seconds.

Within the Library list and the workflow variables area, variables are color-coded to indicate whether they have modifiable options: Blue variables have modifiable options; purple ones do not. Within the Library list, icons are also used to denote whether a variable is customizable: The V icon indicates a customizable variable, and the ⚙ icon indicates a noncustomizable variable (**Figures 8.32** and **8.33**).

To adjust the options for a variable:

1. Double-click the desired variable in the workflow variables area at the bottom of the workflow window.

   A Variable Options window opens (**Figure 8.34**).

2. If you'd like, enter a new name for the variable.

3. Make any changes to the variable's options (**Figure 8.35**).

4. Click Done.

   The Variable Options window closes. When you run the workflow, the variable retrieves its value using the options you specified.

✔ Tip

■ A variable's options are different depending on the variable's function. The *Current time* variable, for example, allows you to specify the format of the retrieved time. The *Path* variable, on the other hand, allows you to specify a custom file or folder path.

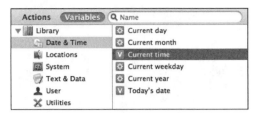

Figure 8.32 Within the Library list, customizable variables are denoted by blue icons, and noncustomizable variables are denoted by purple icons.

Figure 8.33 Within the workflow variables area at the bottom of the workflow window, customizable variables appear blue and noncustomizable variables appear purple.

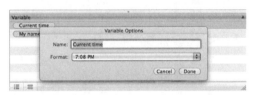

Figure 8.34 Double-click a blue variable in the workflow variables area to display the Variable Options window.

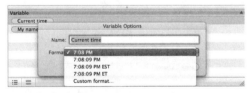

Figure 8.35 In the Variable Options window, you can adjust how the variable behaves when the workflow runs.

Figure 8.36 From the Files & Folders category, drag the New Folder action to the workflow. Do not adjust any of its default settings.

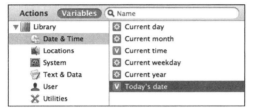

Figure 8.37 Click the Date & Time category to display a list of variables within that category.

Creating a Simple Variable Workflow

A great way to become acquainted with variables is to create a workflow that uses one. This example walks you through creating a very simple workflow using a single pre-defined variable to create a dated folder on the desktop. The example also demonstrates adjusting the variable's options to change the date formatting in the folder's name.

Actions used:

◆ New Folder

Variables used:

◆ *Today's date*

To build the workflow:

1. Create a new custom workflow window.

2. From the Files & Folders category, drag the New Folder action to the workflow area.

   This action is configured to create a folder on your desktop. Do not enter a name into the action's Name field (**Figure 8.36**).

3. At the top of the Library list, click the Variables button.

   A categorized list of variables appears, replacing the categorized list of actions (**Figure 8.37**).

continues on next page

CREATING A SIMPLE VARIABLE WORKFLOW

4. From the Date & Time category, drag the *Today's date* variable into the New Folder action's Name field (**Figure 8.38**).

The variable appears in the Name field of the action, and the workflow variables list is displayed at the bottom of the workflow area (**Figure 8.39**).

✔ Tip

■ Due to an apparent bug in Snow Leopard, running the workflow now produces an error due to the *Today's date* variable containing slash characters. Apparently, the New Folder action doesn't like these. To resolve the problem, you can change the date's format, as you'll learn next.

Figure 8.38 From the Date & Time category, drag the *Today's date* variable to the New Folder action's Name field.

Figure 8.39 The *Today's date* variable now appears in the Name field of the New Folder action as well as in the workflow variables area at the bottom of the workflow window.

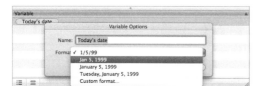

Figure 8.40 Double-click the *Today's date* variable in the workflow variables area to change its format.

Figure 8.41 The New Folder action creates a folder named with the current date on the desktop.

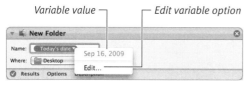

Figure 8.42 When the workflow runs, the value of the *Today's date* variable is indicated in the New Folder action's path pop-up menu.

Changing the Today's date variable format

As you've learned, you can modify the options of some variables. One such variable, *Today's date*, lets you modify the format in which the date is retrieved.

To change the Today's date variable format:

1. In the workflow variables area, double-click the *Today's date* variable.

   The Variable Options window appears. Here you can configure the variable's behavior.

2. If desired, enter a new name for the *Today's date* variable.

3. Choose the desired date format from the Format pop-up menu, such as Jan 5, 1999 (**Figure 8.40**).

4. Click Done.

   The Variable Options window closes.

When you run the workflow, Automator applies your custom date format to the folder created by the New Folder action (**Figure 8.41**). The variable's value may also be verified in the New Folder action's disclosure triangle pop-up menu (**Figure 8.42**).

✔ Tip

- After a workflow has been run, you can also modify an editable variable by clicking its disclosure triangle in a text field or by selecting the variable in a path pop-up menu. When you do this, an Edit option is displayed (Figures 8.31 and 8.42).

CREATING A SIMPLE VARIABLE WORKFLOW

Customizing the Today's date variable

Although the *Today's date* variable has several default formatting options available, you may prefer a more customized format. No problem. You can do that, too.

To customize the Today's date variable:

1. In the workflow variables area, double-click the *Today's date* variable.

   A Variable Options window opens.

2. Choose "Custom format" from the Format pop-up menu.

   The Variable Options window expands to show some additional options, including a customization field and date elements (**Figure 8.43**).

3. Drag the desired date elements into the customization field (**Figure 8.44**).

   For example, to include the month, day, and year, drag the Month, Day of Month, and Year date elements into the customization field.

4. To customize a specific date element, click the triangle on its right within the customization field.

   A contextual menu appears containing several formatting options for the date element (**Figure 8.45**).

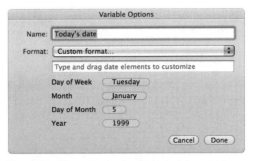

Figure 8.43 To customize the *Today's date* variable, choose "Custom format" from the Format pop-up menu in the Variable Options window.

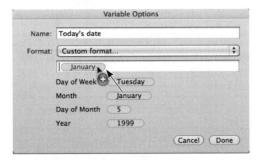

Figure 8.44 Drag the desired date elements to the customization field in the Variable Options window.

Figure 8.45 If desired, click the triangle to the right of each date element in the customization panel to customize its format.

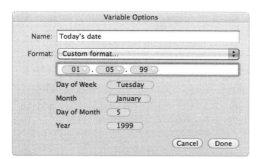

Figure 8.46 The customization field also allows you to enter text to be incorporated with the specified date elements.

Figure 8.47 When the workflow runs, Automator applies the custom format for the *Today's date* variable to the name of the newly created folder.

5. Choose the desired format from the menu.

For example, for the Month date element, you could choose 01 to display the month as a two-digit month.

6. If desired, repeat steps 4 and 5 for any other date elements you've added to the customization panel.

7. If desired, enter into the customization field any text to appear as part of the formatted date, such as a delimiter.

For example, you may want each date element to be separated by a period (**Figure 8.46**).

8. Click Done.

The Variable Options window closes.

Now when you run the workflow, Automator applies your custom date format to the newly created folder (**Figure 8.47**).

✔ Tip

- When you customize a date element's format in the customization field, you may need to click out of the field for the customization to appear onscreen.

Creating an Advanced Variable Workflow

The following example workflow is a bit more advanced. It creates a dated folder on the desktop and then downloads any linked images from the currently opened Safari webpage into that folder. The workflow uses two variables: One retrieves a predefined variable value, and the other stores and retrieves the result of an action within the workflow.

Actions used:

◆ New Folder

◆ Set Value of Variable

◆ Get Current Webpage from Safari

◆ Get Image URLs from Webpage

◆ Download URLs

Variables used:

◆ *Today's date*

◆ *Path*

To build the workflow:

1. Create a new Workflow file.

2. At the top of the Library list, click the Variables button.

   The list of categories and variables displays.

3. In the Date & Time category, double-click the *Today's date* variable.

   The workflow variables area, containing the *Today's date* variable, displays at the bottom of the workflow window (**Figure 8.48**).

4. Double-click the *Today's date* variable in the workflow variables area to display the Variable Options window.

5. Choose the format Jan 5, 1999 (**Figure 8.49**).

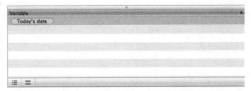

Figure 8.48 From the Date & Time category, add the *Today's date* variable to your workflow.

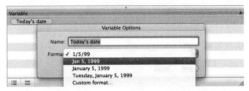

Figure 8.49 Change the *Today's date* variable's format to Jan 5, 1999.

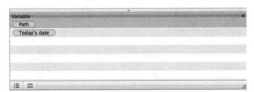

Figure 8.50 From the Locations category, add the *New Path* variable to your workflow.

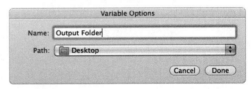

Figure 8.51 Double-click the *New Path* variable in the workflow variables area to display the Variable Options window. Change the name of the variable to *Output Folder*.

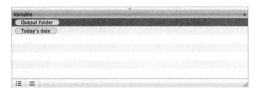

Figure 8.52 The workflow variables area displays a list of the variables you've added to your workflow.

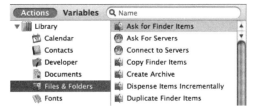

Figure 8.53 Click the Library list's Actions button to display the list of categorized actions.

Figure 8.54 From the Files & Folders category, add a New Folder action to the workflow and enter –Website Photos into the Name field.

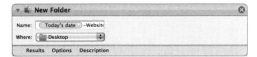

Figure 8.55 Drag the *Today's date* variable to the beginning of the New Folder's Name field.

Figure 8.56 From the Utilities category, add the Set Value of Variable action to the workflow and choose *Output Folder* from the Variable pop-up menu.

6. Click Done.

7. In the Locations category, double-click the *Path* variable.

   The *Path* variable appears in the work-flow variables area (**Figure 8.50**).

8. Double-click the *Path* variable in the workflow variables area.

   The Variable Options window appears.

9. Enter Output Folder into the Name field (**Figure 8.51**).

10. Click Done.

    The Variable Options window closes, and the workflow variables area displays the variable's new name (**Figure 8.52**).

11. At the top of the Library list, click the Actions button.

    The list of categories and actions displays (**Figure 8.53**).

12. From the Files & Folders category, drag the New Folder action to the workflow area.

    Enter –Website Photos into the action's Name field. No additional configuration is necessary (**Figure 8.54**).

13. From the workflow variables area, drag the *Today's date* variable to the beginning of the New Folder action's Name field (**Figure 8.55**).

14. From the Utilities category, drag the Set Value of Variable action to the workflow area.

15. From the action's Variable pop-up menu, choose the *Output Folder* variable (**Figure 8.56**).

continues on next page

CREATING AN ADVANCED VARIABLE WORKFLOW

16. From the Internet category, drag the Get Current Webpage from Safari action to the workflow area (**Figure 8.57**).

17. From the Internet category, drag the Get Image URLs from Webpage action to the workflow area.

18. From the "Get URLs of images" pop-up menu, choose "linked from these webpages" (**Figure 8.58**).

19. From the Internet category, drag the Download URLs action to the workflow area.

20. From the workflow variables area, drag the *Output Folder* variable to the beginning of the Download URLs action's Where pop-up menu (**Figure 8.59**).

The workflow is now complete and ready to be run. It should consist of two variables—*Output Folder* and *Today's date*—and five actions—New Folder, Set Value of Variable, Get Current Webpage from Safari, Get Image URLs from Webpage, and Download URLs (**Figure 8.60**).

Figure 8.57 From the Internet category, add the Get Current Webpage from Safari action to the workflow.

Figure 8.58 From the Internet category, add the Get Image URLs from Webpage action to the workflow and choose "linked from these webpages" from the "Get URLs of images" pop-up menu.

Figure 8.59 From the Internet category, add the Download URLs action to the workflow. Next, drag the *Output Folder* variable from the workflow variables area to the Where pop-up menu.

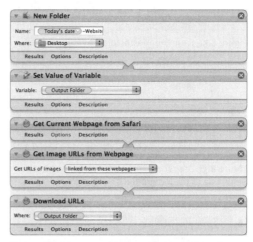

Figure 8.60 The completed workflow consists of five actions: New Folder, Set Value of Variable, Get Current Webpage from Safari, Get Image URLs from Webpage, and Download URLs. Two variables are used throughout this workflow.

CREATING AN ADVANCED VARIABLE WORKFLOW

Figure 8.61 Open a webpage in Safari containing linked images.

Figure 8.62 The value of the *Today's date* variable appears in the variable's contextual menu in the New Folder action.

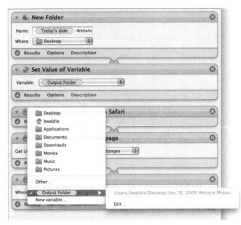

Figure 8.63 The value of the *Output Folder* variable appears in the Download URLs path pop-up menu.

To run the workflow:

1. Launch Safari and go to a webpage containing linked images.

   For this example, you can use my test site at www.automatedworkflows.com/demos/photos/ (**Figure 8.61**).

2. Click the Run button in Automator's toolbar, or press ⌃⌘R.

   The workflow runs. When it's done, the *Today's date* contextual menu in the New Folder action's Name field shows the value of the *Today's date* variable (**Figure 8.62**). The Where pop-up menu in the Download URLs action shows the value of the *Output Folder* variable (**Figure 8.63**). A dated Website Photos folder appears on your desktop containing the downloaded photos (**Figure 8.64**).

Figure 8.64 In this example, a dated Website Photos folder is created on the desktop and contains any downloaded images.

TROUBLESHOOTING

Automator workflows are huge time-savers when they run properly; however, getting them to that point is sometimes easier said than done. Whether you're trying to run an existing workflow or create a new one, at some point you're likely to encounter a problem.

Most problems occur when running workflows, and you usually can resolve them by adjusting action settings. Occasionally, though, you'll encounter problems when opening workflows or even with the Automator application.

Finding and fixing a problem can be a challenge, but this chapter identifies some common problems and walks you through practical steps to help resolve them.

Problems Running Workflows

In general, creating Automator workflows involves a lot of trial and error: configure actions one way, see if the workflow runs, make adjustments, and try the workflow again. Along the way, problems sometimes occur, but when they do, you don't need to panic. Work through each issue slowly, and gradually you'll get the workflow to do what you want.

Step through your workflow

Automator offers the ability to step through your workflow one action at a time rather than running it all at once. In other words, Automator runs an action, and then pauses. While it waits, you are free to check the result of the actions that have run so far, view Automator's log, and more. When you're ready to proceed, Automator runs the next action, and then pauses again.

This is an excellent method of troubleshooting workflow problems! Using this technique, you can move slowly through your workflow, one action at a time, and make sure everything works properly at each step. If you find a problem, stop, fix it, and try again. After you identify and resolve any problems, run the workflow as a whole. If you proceed in this manner, your workflows have a much higher likelihood of running successfully and reliably.

Help for Tiger Users

If you're still using Tiger (Mac OS X 10.4), you can't step through your workflows like a Leopard or Snow Leopard (10.5 or 10.6) user can. You can, however, configure your actions to display when run. Every time an action is displayed, the workflow pauses, allowing you to make sure that the previous action ran successfully.

Figure 9.1 Begin stepping through a workflow by choosing Step from the Workflow menu.

Step button

Figure 9.2 Click the Step button in the toolbar to begin stepping through a workflow.

Action results

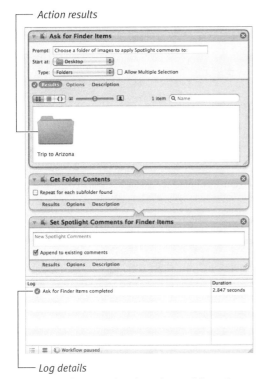

Log details

Figure 9.3 When stepping through a workflow, view the current action's results and the log to see if problems occurred.

To step through your workflow:

1. With a workflow open, choose Workflow > Step (**Figure 9.1**).

   or

   Click the Step button in the workflow window's toolbar (**Figure 9.2**).

   Automator runs the first action in the workflow, and then pauses. While it's paused, check the results of the action and view the log to see if any problems occurred (**Figure 9.3**). Make sure the results are correct, and that the action did what it was supposed to do. For example, if the action creates a folder on the desktop, make sure that the folder was actually created. If the action searches for files, make sure that files were found. Once you determine that the action was successful, you're ready to proceed to the next action.

2. Choose Workflow > Step.

   or

   Click the Step button in the workflow window's toolbar.

   Automator runs the next action, and then pauses again. You can stop stepping through a workflow at any time by choosing Workflow > Stop, clicking Stop in the toolbar, or pressing ⌃⌘.

✔ Tips

- While a workflow is paused, you can change settings in actions that haven't yet run.

- When stepping through a workflow, you can run all remaining actions by choosing Workflow > Run, clicking Run in the toolbar, or pressing ⌃⌘R.

- For Tiger users, I'm afraid you're out of luck. The ability to step through a workflow wasn't added to Automator until Leopard.

- For Leopard users, the Step button wasn't included in Automator's toolbar by default. You can add it by customizing the toolbar.

PROBLEMS RUNNING WORKFLOWS

Troubleshooting a workflow problem

A great way to learn to troubleshoot is to walk through a problem workflow. In this section, you'll create a controlled problematic workflow. You'll then learn how to troubleshoot it by checking action results, checking Automator's log, and more. You can apply these same techniques to troubleshooting real-world workflows.

To create a broken workflow for troubleshooting:

1. Launch iTunes, and choose File > New Playlist to create a new music playlist. Name the playlist My Favorite Songs (**Figure 9.4**).

2. Bring Automator to the front, and create a new Workflow file (**Figure 9.5**).

3. From the Music category, drag the Get Specified iTunes Items action to your workflow.

4. Click the Add button.

   A panel that contains your iTunes songs and playlists appears.

5. When prompted, select the My Favorite Songs playlist and click Add (**Figure 9.6**).

   The My Favorite Songs playlist is added to the Get Specified iTunes Items action.

Figure 9.4 Create a playlist named My Favorite Songs in iTunes.

Figure 9.5 Choose to build a new Workflow file in the template selection panel.

Figure 9.6 Choose the My Favorite Songs playlist when prompted, and click the Add button.

PROBLEMS RUNNING WORKFLOWS

Figure 9.7 A workflow that retrieves a specified playlist from iTunes and plays it.

Figure 9.8 Rename the My Favorite Songs playlist to My Old Favorite Songs in iTunes.

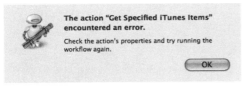

Figure 9.9 Automator displays an error message when an action encounters a problem.

Troubleshooting Different Types of Workflows

If you encounter a problem with a workflow Application, Service, Folder Action, Print Plugin, iCal Alarm, or Image Capture Plugin, open and run it in Automator. You can then step through the workflow, monitor action results, view the log, and more. These capabilities are not available outside of Automator.

---

6. In the Music category of the Library list, click the Play iTunes Playlist action, and drag it to the end of the workflow.

You now have a complete workflow that gets the My Favorite Songs playlist from iTunes and plays it (**Figure 9.7**).

If you run the workflow now, it should run successfully. The purpose of this exercise, however, is to simulate a problem.

7. To create a problem, go back into iTunes, and rename the My Favorite Songs playlist to My Old Favorite Songs (**Figure 9.8**).

8. Run the erroneous workflow.

Automator returns an error. Because the playlist My Favorite Songs was renamed, the Get Specified iTunes Items action can't find it and displays an error message. The message tells you the Get Specified iTunes Items action encountered a problem and suggests checking the action's properties (**Figure 9.9**).

Unfortunately, Automator's error message isn't much help. Therefore, you need to employ some other troubleshooting techniques to find the real source of the problem, specifically:

◆ Check the workflow status.

◆ Check the workflow log.

◆ Check the action results.

✔ Tip

■ When Automator refers to an action's *properties*, it means the action's modifiable settings.

Check the workflow status:

◆ The first place you should check when troubleshooting a workflow is the status area at the bottom of the workflow window. You won't find much information here, but it will tell you if an error occurred (**Figure 9.10**).

Check the workflow log:

◆ Perhaps the most useful way to troubleshoot a problem is to consult Automator's log (choose View > Log or press (Option)(⌘)(L)). Here you can find detailed information about any problems that may have occurred. For the example, the log specifies that iTunes could not locate the My Favorite Songs playlist (**Figure 9.11**).

To resolve this problem, you can rename or re-create the playlist in iTunes. Or, you can reconfigure the Get Specified iTunes Items action to retrieve a different playlist. Either way, you can get the information you need to solve the problem by looking at the log.

Check action results:

◆ To view an action's results, click the Results button at the bottom of the action. The results area for an action that encounters an error appears (**Figure 9.12**). If the action accepts input, however, you may find some clues to what went awry by checking the results of the previous action. You want to make sure that the correct information is passed from the previous action to the action that encountered the error. If it isn't, that may be what's causing the error.

In the example workflow, no actions run before Get Specified iTunes Items, so the results aren't much help.

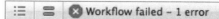

Figure 9.10 The status bar at the bottom of a workflow window indicates when Automator encounters an error.

Figure 9.11 The log is an excellent place to find detailed information about workflow problems. Here the log indicates that iTunes can't locate a playlist named My Favorite Songs.

What's in the Log?

Automator's log provides important information about your workflow, including:

◆ Actions that have run successfully and their durations

◆ Actions that have failed with detailed error messages

◆ Conversion actions that may have run in the background

Refer to the log often, even if you don't receive an error. It may help to shed more light on what's going on as your workflow runs.

Figure 9.12 Check the results of actions in your workflow to help identify potential problems. An action that encounters an error will have no results, but checking the results of previous actions may indicate a problem.

Locating the Culprit Action

When a workflow encounters an error, a red X appears at the bottom of the problematic action. Use this clue to identify where the workflow stopped, and start troubleshooting there.

Checking Action Results in Tiger

Tiger users can check action results by using the View Results action, located under Automator in the Library list. Insert this action throughout your workflow to view the results of any action.

Other troubleshooting techniques

If you can't solve a workflow problem with the techniques just described, try these:

◆ **Make action adjustments.** Consider changing the way the action behaves. Sometimes, a simple adjustment to an action's settings may fix the problem. In the example workflow, you might consider configuring the Get Specified iTunes Items action to display when run, allowing you to choose the playlist at runtime.

◆ **Consider alternate actions.** Some Automator actions do similar tasks, such as Get Specified iTunes Items and Get Selected iTunes Items. Although these actions sound very similar, they work just a bit differently. One allows you to specify iTunes items when you build the workflow. The other gets any selected iTunes items when you run the workflow. If you're encountering a problem with one action, try using another that works in a similar way.

◆ **Disable actions.** Don't forget; you can also disable an action in a workflow. If an action is causing a problem, try disabling it (select the action and choose Action > Disable). See how the workflow runs without the action or with a different action in its place. You can gather some clues from the way the workflow performs at this point. If necessary, you can always enable it again.

Problems Opening Workflows

Not all problems occur when running a workflow: Sometimes just opening one can be problematic. These sorts of issues, however, are generally a bit simpler to diagnose. For the most part, Automator tells you what the problem is.

Missing workflow actions

To open and run a workflow, you must have all actions used by that workflow installed on your machine. Otherwise, Automator displays an error when the workflow is opened (**Figure 9.13**). You're likely to encounter this problem if you're downloading a lot of workflows or getting them from friends.

When this type of error occurs, you can still open the workflow. Any missing actions, however, are dimmed, and their settings are not visible (**Figure 9.14**). In addition, if you try to run the workflow, Automator displays an error message indicating that some actions were not loaded (**Figure 9.15**).

To troubleshoot this problem:

◆ Locate and install the missing action. If you downloaded the workflow, see if the action is available for download, too. Or, if you received the workflow from a friend, ask where you can get the action.

Or

◆ Search the actions you see in Automator's Library list. Perhaps you can locate a similar substitute for the missing one. The workflow might behave slightly differently, but it may still meet your needs.

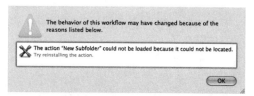

Figure 9.13 Automator notifies you when opening a workflow that uses an action not installed on your machine. For the workflow to run, you must install the missing action.

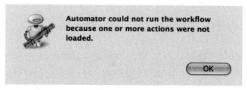

Figure 9.14 A missing workflow action is displayed in Automator, but it's dimmed and its settings are not visible.

Figure 9.15 Automator displays an error message if you try to run a workflow with missing actions.

Action version changes

When an action is upgraded—a new version of the action is released—its behavior or settings may change. For this reason, Automator alerts you when opening a workflow that uses an older version of an action that you have installed. You may need to make some changes to the action's settings so your workflow continues to run successfully (**Figure 9.16**).

When this problem occurs, you can still try running the workflow. In some cases, it may work just fine; in others, however, it may produce an error or not perform as intended. You're likely to encounter this error when opening Tiger workflows in Leopard or Leopard workflows in Snow Leopard, because developers typically upgrade actions when a new operating system is released.

To troubleshoot this problem:

◆ Try running the workflow. If it runs successfully, you're home free!

◆ If the workflow produces an error at runtime, you'll need to configure the action's settings for the newer version. In fact, it's probably best to delete the action from the workflow entirely and insert the new version of the action. This clears any of the action's previously saved settings from the workflow. Once the newer version of the action is inserted, configure it to meet your needs.

continues on next page

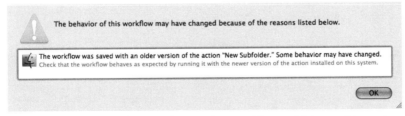

Figure 9.16 Automator notifies you when opening a workflow containing an older version of an action. This is your cue to test the workflow to make sure it still runs smoothly.

PROBLEMS OPENING WORKFLOWS

✔ Tips

- If you're unsure of the latest version available for an action, check the developer's website. If the action has documentation, search it for a version history.

- In Leopard and Snow Leopard, you can view the version of an action in its description area (**Figure 9.17**). The Finder's information window also displays the version number of an action (**Figure 9.18**). Locate and click the action file in the Finder, and choose File > Get Info.

- In Tiger, some developers include version numbers in the action's description area. For others, you'll need to view the action's information window in the Finder.

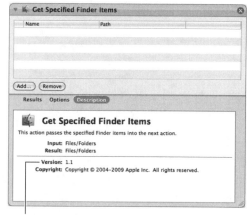

Action version

Figure 9.17 In Leopard, an action's version number is shown in its description.

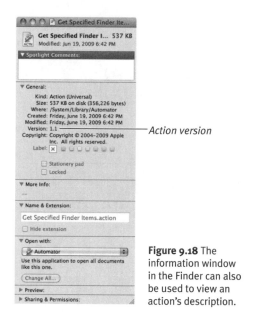

Action version

Figure 9.18 The information window in the Finder can also be used to view an action's description.

Figure 9.19 Automator doesn't always display installed actions. Here, the Photos category lists no iPhoto actions, because iPhoto is not installed.

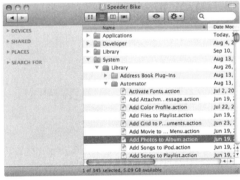

Figure 9.20 The /System/Library/Automator folder contains Automator actions for Apple applications. This example shows that the Add Photos to Album iPhoto action is installed.

General Problems

Most Automator problems are likely to involve opening or running workflows. Occasionally, however, you may encounter some general application-level problems.

Missing actions

Looking for an action in Automator, but just can't seem to find it? Perhaps you saw the action on a friend's machine, but don't see it on yours. There are times when actions may be installed on your system, but don't show up in Automator.

Generally, this problem occurs if you're missing an application required for the action to work. For example, although iPhoto actions may be installed on your machine, if iPhoto isn't installed, Automator won't display the actions (**Figure 9.19**).

To troubleshoot this problem:

1. Make sure that any applications required for the action to work are installed. For example, if the action works with iPhoto, make sure iPhoto is installed.

2. Verify that the action is installed. To do this, look for the action in one of the following folders:

   ▲ **/System/Library/Automator** This folder contains actions for Apple applications that are installed with Mac OS X (**Figure 9.20**). You probably won't find any other actions here.

continues on next page

GENERAL PROBLEMS

Still Not Seeing an Action?

To be visible in Automator, an action sometimes may need a specific version of an application. For example, Automator may not display an action written for Photoshop CS4 if you have Photoshop CS3 installed. Unfortunately, there's no good way to tell which version of an application an action may need. If the action has documentation, check there. If not, try contacting the action's developer.

▲ **/Library/Automator** This folder may contain third-party actions. Actions here are available to all users on your Mac (**Figure 9.21**).

▲ **/Users/YourUserName/Library/ Automator** This folder may also contain third-party actions. Actions here are available to you only, not to other users of your Mac (**Figure 9.22**).

If the problematic action and its required applications are installed on your Mac, the action should be listed in Automator (**Figure 9.23**).

✔ Tips

■ Need help troubleshooting a problem? Check out Chapter 12, "Automator Resources." Here, you'll find links to Automator websites and mailing lists that can be valuable troubleshooting resources.

■ Sometimes, an application may be installed on your machine, but its actions aren't visible in Automator. When this happens, try quitting Automator, launching the application, quitting the application, and relaunching Automator.

■ Automator tries to keep track of the actions installed on your Mac. Sometimes, it can get "stuck," and not show new actions. To resolve the problem, look for variations of files named com.apple.Automator.ActionCache.plist in the ~/Library/Caches folder within your home folder, and delete them. This will clear Automator's cache and cause it to rescan your machine for actions.

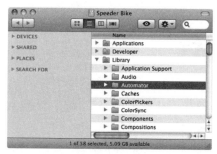

Figure 9.21 Automator actions from third-party developers are sometimes installed in the /Library/Automator folder. Actions in this folder are available to all users of your Mac.

Figure 9.22 Automator actions from third-party developers are also sometimes installed in the /Users/YourUserName/Library/Automator folder. These actions are available to you only, not to other users of your machine.

Figure 9.23 If an action and its required applications are installed on your Mac, you should see the action in Automator.

GENERAL PROBLEMS

CUSTOMIZING AUTOMATOR

Automator is supposed to be easy to use, and as you've seen, most features are easily accessible with a key command or a few mouse clicks. By now you should feel pretty comfortable getting around the interface. You can, however, change the interface's look and feel a bit if you prefer.

As with many other Mac OS X applications, you can reconfigure Automator's toolbar. You can reorder or remove the buttons and add new buttons for frequently accessed features.

Many aspects of the workflow window are also customizable, including whether the Library list is visible, whether the description area is visible, and more. You can even create your own custom groupings of actions and variables. For example, if you frequently use the same actions, you can group them together for quick and easy access, so you don't have to click through different categories to find them.

In this chapter, you'll learn how to adjust Automator's interface to your liking, including adding and removing buttons in the toolbar, resizing the Library list, creating your own custom groups of actions, and more.

Customizing the Toolbar

Even if you're perfectly comfortable using Automator's default toolbar configuration, you may want to consider some customizations. For example, if you regularly print workflows, you can add a button for this task to the toolbar. Or, if you never step through workflows, you might want to remove the Step button from the toolbar.

There's a lot to see in an Automator workflow window; perhaps you'd prefer to reduce the size of the toolbar buttons to gain more screen area to edit your workflows. In this section, you'll learn several ways of customizing Automator's toolbar.

To customize the toolbar:

1. Open a workflow window.

2. Choose View > Customize Toolbar (**Figure 10.1**).

   or

   While holding down the (Control) key, click the toolbar to display the contextual menu, and then choose Customize Toolbar (**Figure 10.2**).

   A customization panel drops down from the toolbar, containing a variety of options, including new buttons, sizing choices, and more (**Figure 10.3**).

3. Make your desired changes to the toolbar, such as adding or removing a button (see the following section for how to do this).

4. Click Done.

   The customization panel closes.

Automator remembers your toolbar customizations and displays them in workflow windows from now on.

Figure 10.1 Choose View > Customize Toolbar from the menu bar to customize Automator's toolbar.

Figure 10.2 You can also customize the toolbar by holding down the (Control) key and clicking on the toolbar. Choose Customize Toolbar from the resulting contextual menu.

Figure 10.3 When you customize Automator's toolbar, a panel appears, giving you access to new buttons and resizing options.

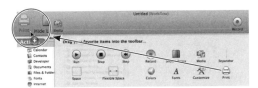

Figure 10.4 To add a button to the toolbar, drag a button from the customization panel to the desired location in the toolbar.

Figure 10.5 When adding a new button to the toolbar, existing buttons move out of the way, if necessary, to make room.

Adding and removing toolbar buttons

Automator makes it easy to add or remove buttons in the toolbar and even provides a way to reset the toolbar to its default buttons.

To add a toolbar button:

1. Follow the steps in the previous section to display the toolbar customization panel.

2. Drag the desired button from the customization panel to the toolbar (**Figure 10.4**).

   Automator moves any existing buttons out of the way by shifting them to the left or right and adds the new button to the toolbar.

Now the button is available for you to use whenever you need it (**Figure 10.5**).

✔ Tip

■ Need to change the location of a button in the toolbar? No problem. With the toolbar customization panel visible, simply click the button and drag it to the desired location. Without the customization panel visible, press ⌘, click the button, and drag it to the desired location.

CUSTOMIZING THE TOOLBAR

To remove a toolbar button:

◆ With the customization panel displayed, drag the button you want to remove off the toolbar. With a puff of smoke, the button disappears (**Figure 10.6**).

or

Without the customization panel displayed, hold down ⌃ ⌘, and drag the button off the toolbar. Again, one puff of smoke, and the button is gone.

or

Without the customization panel displayed, hold down the (Control) key, and click the button within the toolbar to display a contextual menu. Then choose Remove Item from the menu (**Figure 10.7**). Automator removes the button.

To reset the toolbar buttons:

1. Display the toolbar customization panel.

2. Drag the default set of buttons to the toolbar (**Figure 10.8**).

   Any buttons you've added are removed, and the default buttons are displayed again (**Figure 10.9**).

Figure 10.6 When customizing the toolbar, remove a button by simply dragging it off the toolbar.

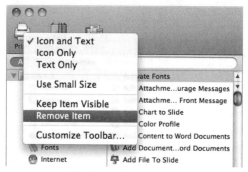

Figure 10.7 A toolbar button can also be removed by choosing Remove Item from the contextual menu. To display the contextual menu, hold down (Control) and click the toolbar.

Figure 10.8 To reset the toolbar, simply drag the default set of buttons from the customization panel to the toolbar.

Figure 10.9 When you drag the default set of buttons to the toolbar, any buttons you've added disappear and the original buttons are displayed.

Figure 10.10 The toolbar buttons at their normal, large size.

Figure 10.11 The toolbar buttons at their reduced size.

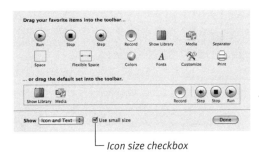

Icon size checkbox

Figure 10.12 Click the Use Small Size checkbox to reduce the size of the buttons in the toolbar and gain slightly more space to build your workflows.

Figure 10.13 Reduce the size of toolbar buttons by choosing Use Small Size from the contextual menu. To display this menu, hold down [Control] and click the toolbar.

Resizing toolbar buttons

The buttons in Automator's toolbar can be viewed in two sizes: small and large (**Figures 10.10** and **10.11**). Unless you have a lot of buttons in the toolbar, the default size of large is probably just fine. You can, however, change the size if you prefer.

To change the size of toolbar buttons:

1. Display the toolbar customization panel.

2. Click the "Use small size" checkbox (**Figure 10.12**).

Or

1. Hold down [Control] and click the toolbar to display the contextual menu (**Figure 10.13**).

2. Choose Use Small Size from the menu.

To enlarge the buttons, deselect the "Use small size" checkbox in the customization panel, or deselect the Use Small Size menu item in the contextual menu.

Changing the style of toolbar buttons

By default, toolbar buttons are displayed as icons with text below them. If you want to maximize the amount of space available for creating workflows, you can display them as icons only or, even better, as text only. You won't gain a huge amount of extra space, but every little bit can help (**Figures 10.14**, **10.15**, and **10.16**).

To change the style of the toolbar buttons:

1. Display the toolbar customization panel.

2. From the pop-up menu at the bottom of the customization panel, choose Icon and Text, Icon Only, or Text Only (**Figure 10.17**).

Or

1. Hold down Control and click the toolbar to display the contextual menu.

2. Choose Icon and Text, Icon Only, or Text Only (**Figure 10.18**).

   Automator updates the buttons in the toolbar to reflect the chosen style.

Congratulations! You now have a few millimeters of extra space to build your workflows.

Figure 10.14 By default, toolbar buttons are displayed as icons and text.

Figure 10.15 To reduce the size of the toolbar ever so slightly, display toolbar buttons as icons only.

Figure 10.16 For the most screen real estate, display toolbar buttons as text only.

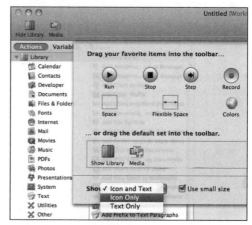

Figure 10.17 To change the style of buttons, choose from the pop-up menu at the bottom of the customization panel.

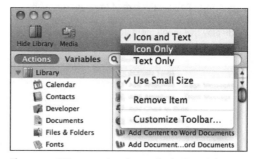

Figure 10.18 You can also change the button style using the toolbar's contextual menu. Hold down Control and click the toolbar to display the contextual menu.

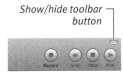

Show/hide toolbar button

Figure 10.19 To hide the toolbar, click the oval-shaped button in its upper-right corner.

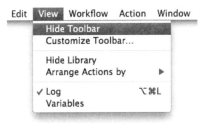

Figure 10.20 Hiding the toolbar from Automator's menu bar.

Hiding the toolbar

Because many of the buttons in the toolbar have corresponding keyboard shortcuts, you may not need to see the toolbar all the time. As you get more comfortable with Automator, you may start relying on keyboard shortcuts more and more. If you find you are not using the toolbar much, you can hide it from view entirely.

To hide the toolbar:

◆ Click the oval-shaped button in the upper right of the toolbar (**Figure 10.19**).

or

Choose View > Hide Toolbar (**Figure 10.20**).

The toolbar disappears, giving you more room to edit your workflow (**Figure 10.21**).

To display the toolbar again, click the oval-shaped button in the upper right of the work-flow window, or choose View > Show Toolbar.

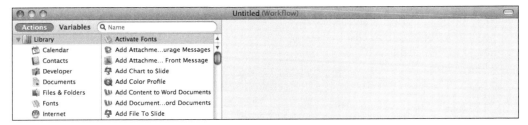

Figure 10.21 With the toolbar hidden, only the title of the workflow is visible at the top of the window. Now there's more room to edit your workflow.

CUSTOMIZING THE TOOLBAR

Customizing the Workflow Window

The toolbar isn't the only interface element that's customizable in Automator. You can also change how the workflow window appears and functions. For example, you can resize the Library list or hide it entirely, hide the description area, show the log, and more.

✔ Tip

■ When you make changes to a new workflow window, Automator automatically applies those changes to future windows. For example, resizing a new workflow window causes future windows to be created at the new size.

Resizing the Library list

Action names are sometimes lengthy, causing them to appear cropped in the Library list. This can make it tough to find the action you're looking for. To reduce cropping, you can expand the size of the Library list.

To resize the Library list:

◆ Click the ▥ handle in the lower right of the Library list, beneath the description area, and drag it to the left or right to the desired width.

or

Click and drag the divider line between the Library list and the workflow area to the left or the right to the desired width.

or

Click and drag the divider line between the columns of the Library list to the left or right to change the width of the indi- vidual columns.

or

Click and drag the divider line between the Library list and the description area to the desired height (**Figure 10.22**).

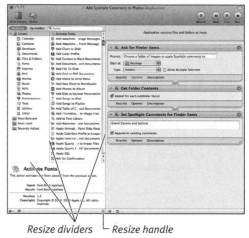

Resize dividers — Resize handle

Figure 10.22 To prevent action names from appearing cropped, you can adjust the size of the Library list.

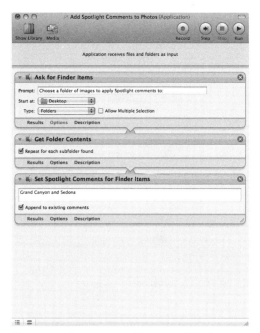

Figure 10.23 Automator enables you to hide the Library list entirely, giving you more room to view and edit your workflow.

Hiding the Library list

When you finish adding actions to a workflow, you may not need to use the Library list again for a while. To give yourself more room to edit the actions in the workflow, you can hide the Library list (**Figure 10.23**).

To hide the Library list:

◆ Click the Hide Library button in the toolbar (**Figure 10.24**).

or

Choose View > Hide Library (**Figure 10.25**).

The workflow area expands to the left, hiding the Library list. Now you can focus your attention on the actions in your workflow without getting distracted by unneeded interface elements.

You can make the Library list visible by clicking Show Library in the toolbar or by choosing View > Show Library (**Figure 10.26**).

Figure 10.24 Click the Hide Library button in the toolbar to hide the Library list.

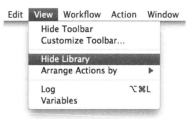

Figure 10.25 Choosing View > Hide Library to hide the Library list.

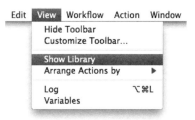

Figure 10.26 Choosing View > Show Library to view the Library list again.

CUSTOMIZING THE WORKFLOW WINDOW

231

Hiding the description area

As you become more familiar with Automator actions, you may not need the description area as often. You may want to hide it.

To hide the description area:

◆ Click the ▾ button in the bottom left of the workflow window.

The description area disappears, and the Library list now takes up the entire left side of the workflow window (**Figure 10.27**).

To redisplay the description area, click the ▣ button in the bottom left of the workflow window.

✔ Tip

■ With the description area hidden, you can still view the description of an individual action within your workflow by clicking the Description button at the bottom of the action.

Showing the log area

As you know, the log is a valuable tool for troubleshooting workflow problems. It's wise to make it visible, so you can identify any problems right away.

To show the log area:

◆ Click the ≣ button beneath the workflow area (**Figure 10.28**).

   or

   Choose View > Log (**Figure 10.29**).

   or

   Press Option ⌃ ⌘ L.

   The log area appears, allowing you to monitor the progress of your workflow as it runs within Automator.

✔ Tip

■ For more on using the log, see Chapter 9, "Troubleshooting."

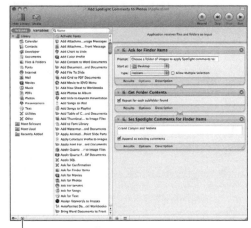

⌐ *Hide/show description button*

Figure 10.27 The description area beneath the Library list can be hidden from view to gain more room for the list of available actions.

⌐ *Show/hide log button*

Figure 10.28 The log is a valuable troubleshooting tool. Consider keeping it visible at the bottom of your workflow window at all times.

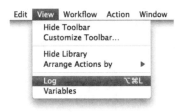

Figure 10.29 To display the log choose View > Log or press Option ⌃ ⌘ L.

CUSTOMIZING THE WORKFLOW WINDOW

Show/hide workflow variables button

Figure 10.30 The workflow variables area allows you to monitor the values of variables used throughout your workflow.

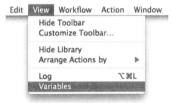

Figure 10.31
Choose View > Variables to display the workflow variables area.

Showing the workflow variables area

If your workflow uses variables, you may want to view them in a list. To do this, you can display a workflow variables area beneath the main workflow area (**Figure 10.30**).

To show the workflow variables area:

◆ Click the ▤ button at the bottom of the workflow area.

or

Choose View > Variables (**Figure 10.31**).

The workflow variables area appears, allowing you to monitor the values of the variables used in your workflow as it runs within Automator.

✔ Tip

■ For more on creating, using, and monitoring variables, see Chapter 8, "Using Variables."

CUSTOMIZING THE WORKFLOW WINDOW

Grouping Actions

The Library list's categories and search field make it easy to locate an action with only a few mouse clicks. If you find you are using the same actions repeatedly, however, you may want to avoid having to click through these categories or enter a search term. Instead, you may want an easier way to access the actions and to differentiate them from other actions you don't use as often.

In Mac OS X, many applications allow you to customize how you organize items. In the Finder, you can store files in folders. In iPhoto, you can add photos to albums. In iTunes, you can create playlists of songs. Automator is no different: In it, you can create custom action groups. For example, you might want to create a group for any third-party actions you've installed or for the actions you use most often (**Figure 10.32**).

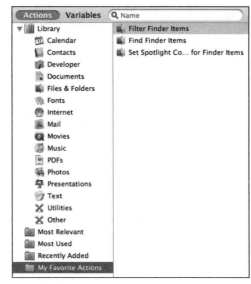

Figure 10.32 To easily find the actions you use most often, organize them into custom groups.

Figure 10.33 To create a custom group of actions, choose New Group from the pop-up menu in the bottom left of the workflow window.

Figure 10.34 A newly created custom group, ready to be renamed to identify the actions it contains.

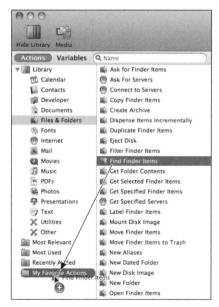

Figure 10.35 To add actions to a custom group, find them and drag them to the group.

To create a custom group of actions:

1. In the bottom left of the workflow window, click the ⚙▾ button to display a pop-up menu.

2. From the pop-up menu, choose New Group (**Figure 10.33**).

   Automator creates an empty group at the bottom of the Library list, leaving the group's name selected.

3. Enter a name for the group, such as My Favorite Actions (**Figure 10.34**).

4. Find the actions you want to add and drag them to your custom group (**Figure 10.35**).

You now have a grouping of custom actions, which you can quickly access when creating workflows. In addition to residing within the group, the actions still reside within their original categories.

✔ Tip

- You can create groups of variables in the same way you can group actions.

To remove a custom group:

1. Select the custom group in the Library list.

2. Press Delete.

or

From the pop-up menu in the lower left of the workflow window, choose Remove Groups (**Figure 10.36**).

Automator asks if you really want to remove the group.

3. Click OK to remove the group, or click Cancel to retain the group (**Figure 10.37**).

✔ Tip

■ Removing a group deletes the group only, not the actions within it. The actions remain listed in their original locations as well.

Creating smart groups of actions

Many Mac OS X applications enable you to create smart groups, which are essentially saved searches matching criteria that you specify. For example, iPhoto allows you to create smart albums of photos, such as any photo assigned the keyword "Vacation." In iTunes, you can create smart playlists of songs, such as any song recorded in the 1960s. In the Finder, you can create smart folders of items, such as any item whose modification date is in the current week. In Automator, you can create smart groups, too—smart groups of actions.

Unlike with custom groups of actions, you don't need to add anything into a smart group. Rather, you enter the desired search criteria, and then Automator automatically finds all actions matching those criteria. For example, you might create a smart group that finds all actions that accept text as input.

Figure 10.36 To remove a group, select the group and choose Remove Groups from the pop-up menu in the lower right of the workflow area.

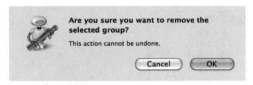

Figure 10.37 Automator makes sure you don't accidentally remove a group by displaying an alert asking for confirmation.

Figure 10.38 Smart groups display actions that meet specific criteria. The Most Used smart group displays the 25 actions you use most often.

Figure 10.39 To create a smart group, choose New Smart Group from the pop-up menu in the lower left of the workflow window.

Several smart groups already exist in Automator's Library list (**Figure 10.38**):

◆ **Most Relevant.** Displays a list of actions that are most relevant to the actions within your workflow. As you add more actions to your workflow, the list of relevant actions is updated.

◆ **Most Used.** Displays a list of the 25 actions you use most often.

◆ **Recently Added.** Displays a list of the 25 most recently added actions within the last 14 days. If you haven't installed new actions on your machine, this list is empty.

To add a smart group:

1. From the pop-up menu at the bottom-left corner of the workflow window, choose New Smart Group (**Figure 10.39**).

   Automator displays a panel in which you can specify the desired search criteria.

2. In the Name field, enter a name for the smart group.

3. In the criteria area, choose the search criteria you want to use to fill the smart group. For example, suppose you use Mail and iCal to create most of your workflows. You can configure the smart group to display any actions that interact with those applications.

4. To reduce the number of actions that fill the smart group, click the "Limit number of items to" checkbox and enter a limit value in the text field.

continues on next page

5. From the "Sort by" pop-up menu, choose how you'd like the actions to be sorted within the smart group. By default, actions are sorted by name.

6. Click OK (**Figure 10.40**).

Automator creates a smart group at the bottom of the Library list. Click the group to display any actions matching the criteria you specified (**Figure 10.41**).

When you create a smart group, you're not locked in. You can change it in the future, if necessary, by modifying its search criteria or adding new criteria.

✔ Tips

■ You cannot create a smart group for variables.

■ To remove a smart group, follow the instructions earlier in this chapter for removing a custom group. The same steps apply to smart groups.

To edit a smart group:

1. Click the smart group in the Library list.

2. Choose Edit Group from the pop-up menu in the bottom left of the workflow window.

Automator displays the smart group configuration panel again; you can then make any desired changes (**Figure 10.42**).

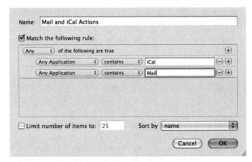

Figure 10.40 When configuring a smart group, specify the desired search criteria.

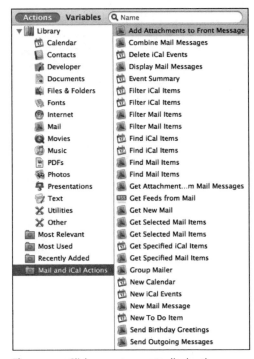

Figure 10.41 Click a smart group to display the actions matching the group's specified search criteria.

Figure 10.42 To edit a smart group, select the group in the Library list. Then choose Edit Group from the pop-up menu in the bottom left of the Library list.

SHARING ACTIONS AND WORKFLOWS

Automator is a truly amazing technology that can benefit virtually every Mac user. Unfortunately, people are often intimidated by it and are unsure of how to get started. But you can help spread the good word about Automator by showing others what it can do and how easy it is to use. If you've created a useful workflow, send it to friends so they can use it too. Once they've seen the benefits of Automator firsthand, they're sure to begin adopting it.

This chapter explores various ways of sharing actions and workflows with friends and colleagues, including emailing workflows, locating action files in the Finder, importing actions on your own machine, and printing workflows.

Distributing Workflows

Automator workflows that have been saved as Applications or Workflow files are just like any other file on the Mac. They can be moved or copied anywhere on your machine, and they can also be sent to other users.

Other types of workflows

You can also send Service, Folder Action, Print Plugin, iCal Alarm, and Image Capture Plugin workflows to others. You just need to know where to find them, and the other person needs to know where to install them for use.

◆ **Service** workflows are in ~/Library/ Services.

◆ **Folder Action** workflows are in ~/Library/Workflows/Applications/ Folder Actions.

◆ **Print Plugin** workflows are in ~/Library/ PDF Services.

◆ **iCal Alarm** workflows are in ~/Library/ Workflows/Applications/iCal.

◆ **Image Capture Plugin** workflows are in ~/Library/Workflows/Applications/ Image Capture.

✔ Tips

- When you send one of these types of workflows to others, be sure to let them know the type of workflow and where to install it.

- When you send a Folder Action workflow to others, they need to attach it to a folder on their machine. They should open the workflow in Automator and attach it to a folder. Or, press (Control) and click on the folder to display the Finder's contextual menu. Then use Folder Actions Setup to attach the workflow to the folder.

- When you send an iCal Alarm workflow to others, they need to create an event in iCal and add an Open File alarm to the event. They should direct the Open File alarm to the installed workflow.

- Remember, ~ means the folder resides within your home folder.

DISTRIBUTING WORKFLOWS

Emailing workflows

Probably the simplest way to distribute work-flows is to send them as email attachments. Just be sure that the recipients have installed the correct versions of the actions required by the workflow. Otherwise, as mentioned in Chapter 9, "Troubleshooting," they will get an error message when opening or running the workflow indicating that required actions cannot be found. If a user doesn't have the required actions, consider sending them as well.

✔ Tip

■ To minimize file size and reduce the possibility of corruption, archive workflows when emailing them to friends. To archive a workflow as a zip file, select it in the Finder and choose File > Compress *<name of file>*, or press (Control), click on the file, and choose Compress *<name of file>*.

Publicly distributing workflows

If you've created a really useful workflow, you may want to make it available to a larger audience. As you'll learn in Chapter 12, "Automator Resources," there are a number of websites that cater to hosting user-contributed workflows, including Apple's own Mac OS X Downloads site (www.apple.com/downloads/macosx/automator/) and MacScripter (http://macscripter.net). Feel free to submit your workflow for inclusion on one of these sites.

Action distribution limitations

Treat Automator actions like any software application. Although many third-party actions are available as freeware, some may be commercial. Keep this in mind, and before sending an action to a friend or colleague, consult the action's documentation. If a license is included, make sure you won't violate it by distributing the action. If the license restricts distribution or is unclear, consider sending the recipient a URL to the developer's website instead.

Locating Action Files

If you intend to send an action to a friend or colleague, you need to find it first. Because actions can be located within an application's bundle or within one of several folders on your Mac, this can sometimes be a challenge.

Where action files reside

As mentioned previously, an action can reside in one of several locations on your machine:

◆ **Application bundle.** Some applications don't store their actions in a folder. Rather, the actions are included within the application. When Automator launches, it scans the bundled applications on your Mac and looks for actions like these. Some third-party Automator action packs are applications containing embedded actions.

◆ **/System/Library/Automator.** This folder contains actions for applications installed with Mac OS X, such as iCal, Mail, and TextEdit. It's highly unlikely that third-party actions would ever be in this folder.

◆ **/Library/Automator.** This folder is the most likely location to hold third-party actions that you installed. Any actions contained within this folder are available to all user accounts on your machine.

◆ **~/Library/Automator.** This folder may also contain third-party actions. Any actions in this folder are available to you only, not to other user accounts.

Although you can certainly spend time scanning these locations for an action, Automator provides a much easier way to find the one you're looking for.

What's a Bundle?

A bundle is a directory in Mac OS X that contains a group of related files and folders. Often, bundles are "packaged" to look like a single file to the user. Many applications in Mac OS X are packaged bundles, containing components necessary for the application to function. When you double-click a bundled application, executable code within the bundle runs and the application launches.

To locate an action file using Automator:

1. In an opened workflow, select an action in the workflow area.

2. Choose Action > Show in Finder (**Figure 11.1**).

   or

   Press ⌃Control⌃, and click the title bar of the action. From the resulting contextual menu, choose Show in Finder (**Figure 11.2**).

   The Finder comes to the front and a new window opens, displaying the selected action (**Figure 11.3**).

✔ Tip

- This procedure works even for actions embedded within an application's bundle.

Figure 11.1 To locate an action's file in the Finder, select the action in your workflow and then choose Action > Show in Finder.

Figure 11.2 To locate an action's file in the Finder, choose Show in Finder from the contextual menu.

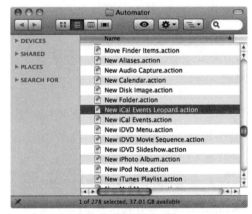

Figure 11.3 When you choose to show an action in the Finder, a new window opens, displaying the selected action.

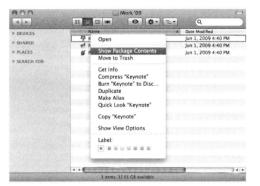

Figure 11.4 To display the contents of a bundled application, choose Show Package Contents from the application's contextual menu.

Figure 11.5 Actions stored within an application's bundle are in the bundle's /Contents/Library/ Automator folder. This example shows the actions within Keynote's bundle.

To manually locate actions within an application's bundle:

1. Find the application that may contain the action you want.

   This example uses Keynote, which contains embedded actions within its bundle.

2. Press Control, and click the application in the Finder to display the contextual menu.

3. Choose Show Package Contents from the menu (**Figure 11.4**).

   A new Finder window opens and displays the contents of the application's bundle. If the application contains Automator actions, they can be found in the bundle's /Contents/Library/Automator folder (**Figure 11.5**).

✔ Tip

■ This example is meant only to show you where actions reside within an application's bundle. It's not recommended to remove actions, or any other components for that matter, from an application's bundle.

LOCATING ACTION FILES

Importing Actions

Sharing Automator workflows is a two-way street. In addition to distributing workflows you've created, you may also receive workflows from others or download them from the Web. To run workflows that you've acquired, you must first install any required third-party actions.

As you've learned, some actions are installed within applications. For these, you just need to install the required application; you'll need it anyway for the workflow to function.

Some third-party actions may come with a stand-alone action installer. Simply run it to automatically install the actions into the correct location on your machine.

Of course, you can also manually install actions by moving them into one of the /Library/Automator folders on your machine—at the root level of your hard drive for all users on your machine or within your user folder for you only.

Actions can also be installed from within Automator. If you're installing actions that don't have an installer of their own, use this method.

✔ Tips

- You may need to relaunch Automator to see third-party actions you've installed.

- Remember, you may also need to configure a workflow someone sends you or install it in a specific location.

IMPORTING ACTIONS

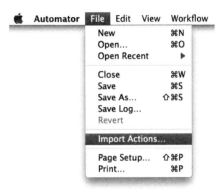

Figure 11.6 To import third-party actions into Automator, choose File > Import Actions.

To import third-party action files from within Automator:

1. Choose File > Import Actions (**Figure 11.6**).

   An Import Automator Action window appears.

2. Locate and choose the actions you want to import.

3. Click Import (**Figure 11.7**).

   The chosen actions are imported into the ~/Library/Automator folder within your home folder (**Figure 11.8**).

There's no need to relaunch Automator this time. Assuming you have any applications and other resources required by the imported actions, you should see the new actions in Automator's Library list immediately. Go ahead and begin adding them to your workflows (**Figure 11.9**).

Figure 11.7 When prompted, locate the actions you want to import and click Import.

Figure 11.8 Imported actions are added to the ~/Library/Automator folder. They are available only for you, not in other user accounts on your machine.

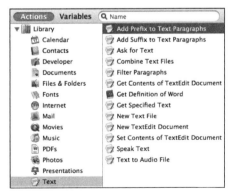

Figure 11.9 Imported actions appear in Automator right away, assuming any required applications are installed.

IMPORTING ACTIONS

Printing a Workflow

Another way to share workflows with others is in print format. One advantage of sharing a printed workflow is that it doesn't require recipients to have the workflow's actions installed. In fact, they don't even need to have a Mac! You may just want to show off to some of your PC buddies at work.

Printing a workflow can also be helpful when you are creating a workflow. It allows you to place the entire workflow on paper right in front of you, which may be useful when working with lengthy workflows. You can then review the actions and their settings simultaneously to ensure that all are configured properly. You can also consider potential areas for improvement or additional actions that you may want to add to the workflow.

To print a workflow:

1. Open the workflow.

2. Choose File > Print (**Figure 11.10**).

   or

   Press ⌃ ⌘ P.

   A print panel appears attached to the workflow window (**Figure 11.11**).

3. Click Print.

   The workflow prints.

A printed workflow shows what you see onscreen when viewing the workflow in Automator—previews of all the workflow's actions, including their settings (**Figure 11.12**).

✔ Tips

- To modify the page setup prior to printing, choose File > Page Setup or press ⇧Shift ⌃ ⌘ P.

- To save the workflow as a PDF, choose Save as PDF from the PDF menu at the bottom of the print panel.

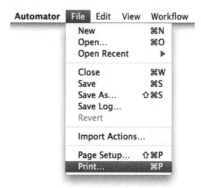

Figure 11.10 To print an open workflow in Automator, choose File > Print or press ⌃ ⌘ P.

Figure 11.11 When printing a workflow, a print panel is displayed attached to the workflow. Here, you can specify the target printer and adjust other print options.

Figure 11.12 A printed workflow shows previews of all the actions within the workflow.

AUTOMATOR RESOURCES

You're now ready to begin using Automator on your own. Along the way, you may encounter obstacles or questions. Remain calm. Loads of available resources can help you through tough situations and take you to the next level with Automator.

Numerous websites provide detailed Automator information, such as tutorials, tips, and example workflows. Hundreds of third-party actions are available for download, enabling you to expand the list of actions installed on your machine. Mailing lists and forums provide an excellent opportunity to meet other Automator users, ask questions, and find answers.

This chapter provides a comprehensive list of these and other valuable Automator resources. Of course, be sure to keep this book handy, too, and use it regularly as a quick reference guide for creating workflows, looping, using variables, and more.

Automator's Help

Like many applications in Mac OS X, Automator contains built-in help documentation. You can use it while building your workflows to find basic information about actions, variables, workflows, and other important topics.

Figure 12.1 Choose Help > Automator Help to display Automator's help documentation.

To access Automator's help documentation:

1. Choose Help > Automator Help (**Figure 12.1**).

   A window appears, displaying Automator's help documentation.

2. Browse the topics listed, or enter a query into the search field in the window's toolbar (**Figure 12.2**).

Figure 12.2 Automator's help documentation provides quick access to basic information about workflows, actions, and more.

Figure 12.3 Choose Help > Open Examples Folder to display the example workflows that are installed with Mac OS X.

Figure 12.4 Automator's example workflows provide a good starting point for working with Automator. Open them, see how they work, and adjust them to meet your needs.

Automator's Example Workflows

An excellent way to learn Automator is to look at examples of completed workflows. Although you can find numerous example workflows online, Apple includes a few with Automator to get you started. You're encouraged to open these workflows and study them to see how they work. Use them to get ideas for your own workflows, and don't be afraid to adjust them to meet your needs.

To view Automator's example workflows:

1. Choose Help > Open Examples Folder (**Figure 12.3**).

    or

    Open /Library/Application Support/ Apple/Automator/Workflows/.

    The Workflows folder opens to display several example workflows (**Figure 12.4**).

2. Double-click the desired workflow to open it in Automator.

    You can study the workflow, modify it, or run it.

Websites

Although Mac OS X includes hundreds of
actions, and even more are bundled with
Apple and third-party applications, these
actions don't do everything. Fortunately, hundreds of additional actions—and the list is
constantly growing—are available for download from third-party developers. Although
some of these actions are available commer-
cially, you can download many for free.

For an excellent way to jump-start your
adoption of Automator, check out the loads
of prebuilt workflows online. Before building
a workflow, consider looking for an existing
one to use as is or modify to meet your needs.

The following websites are excellent resources
for learning more about Automator, as well
as expanding your library of actions and
workflows.

Mac OS X Automation

www.macosxautomation.com

This website is the definitive resource
for all things Automator. Here, you'll find
Automator tips, tricks, tutorials, and videos,
as well as downloadable actions, workflows,
and much more. This website is updated
often, so be sure to check it regularly.

Apple's Mac OS X Downloads

*www.apple.com/downloads/macosx/
automator/*

Apple's Mac OS X Downloads website is
an excellent resource that contains an
entire category specifically for third-party
Automator actions and workflows. Of course,
you'll find lots of other great downloads
here as well, including Mac applications,
Dashboard widgets, and much more.

The Companion Website

*www.peachpit.com/vqs/automator-
snow-leopard*

Visit the companion website for this book
to access downloadable versions of the
example workflows, as well as any errata
information that may be provided in the
future.

See page 258 for details.

MacScripter

http://macscripter.net

Although the primary focus of this website is AppleScript, you'll also find a wealth of information here about Automator, such as articles and links. An Automator Actions section also includes hundreds of downloadable actions and workflows.

Mac OS X Automator Video Training

By Jesse Feiler

www.vtc.com/products/Mac-OS-X-Automator -tutorials.htm

VTC (Virtual Training Company) offers a ton of high-quality Mac-related video tutorials, including a course on Automator. The first three chapters of this course are available online for free viewing, or you can purchase the complete course as a CD or via VTC's Online University.

✔ Tip

- VTC's Online University gives you unlimited access to hundreds of video tutorials, making it an excellent way to get low cost video-based training.

Peachpit Press Articles, Blogs, and Podcasts

www.peachpit.com/benwaldie

I've written dozens of articles and blog entries about Automator for Peachpit Press, and they're all available online for free. Simply visit my author page on the Peachpit website for a comprehensive list.

www.peachpit.com/macautomation

My video podcast series, *Mac Automation Made Simple*, provides step-by-step video tutorials on Automator and AppleScript. You can also find the series on the Peachpit website above or in the podcast section of the iTunes Music Store.

Automated Workflows, LLC

www.automatedworkflows.com/tips/tips.html

This is the Tips section of my website. Here, you'll find links to numerous Automator tutorials and articles that I've written for Apple. com, *Macworld* magazine, Peachpit Press, and more. If you're interested in expanding your automation skills, be sure to check out some of my AppleScript articles for *MacTech*, MacScripter, and others while you're there.

www.automatedworkflows.com/software/ automator_actions.html

I have released hundreds of shareware Automator actions for such applications as FileMaker Pro, Illustrator, InDesign, Photoshop, and QuarkXPress, among others. Visit my website to download trial versions of these actions, access example workflows, and more.

WEBSITES

Mailing Lists and Forums

User-to-user support is perhaps the best way to receive quick Automator assistance when you need it, and several mailing lists and forums are available to help. Typically, these resources are host to hundreds if not thousands of other users who are usually more than happy to provide a quick answer to any question you may have. Participant skill level varies from extreme novice to super geek, so don't be afraid to ask a question, no matter how simple or complex it may seem. As you become an expert on Automator, don't forget to share your expertise, too.

Apple's Automator Users Mailing List

http://lists.apple.com/mailman/listinfo/automator-users

Many people may be unaware that Apple provides mailing lists for dozens of applications and Mac-related topics, including Aperture, QuickTime, and—you guessed it—Automator. These mailing lists provide an excellent opportunity to network with other Mac users, as well as get quick answers to your burning questions. Automator even includes menu items to aid you in signing up and sending messages to others on this valuable list.

To join the Automator Users Mailing List:

1. Choose Help > Join Automator Mailing List (**Figure 12.5**).

   The Automator Users Mailing List webpage opens in your web browser.

2. Enter your name, email address, and a password, and follow the instructions to subscribe (**Figure 12.6**).

   You are sent an email requesting confirmation of your subscription.

Figure 12.5 Choose Help > Join Automator Mailing List to open a subscription page in your web browser.

Figure 12.6 Apple's website allows you to subscribe to dozens of Mac-related mailing lists, including the Automator Users Mailing list.

After confirming your subscription, you will receive regular emails from other users subscribed to the list. Feel free to email your own Automator-related questions to the list, and be sure to answer questions from others if you are able to do so.

✔ Tips

- To reduce the number of emails you receive, subscribe to the list as a daily digest.

- Consider setting up a mail rule to auto-filter mailing list emails into a specific mailbox, allowing you to review them at your leisure.

- You can manage your mailing list subscription or unsubscribe from the Automator Users Mailing List webpage at http://lists.apple.com/mailman/listinfo/automator-users.

To email the Automator User's Mailing List:

1. Choose Help > Send Mail to Automator Mailing List.

   A new email message is created, addressed to the mailing list.

2. Type a subject and your question, and send the email.

   Now, just sit back and wait for a response.

✔ Tip

- For help with other Apple technologies, check out the other mailing lists available at http://lists.apple.com/.

MAILING LISTS AND FORUMS

Apple's Automator discussion boards

http://discussions.apple.com

If you prefer not to clutter your inbox with email from a mailing list, Apple also offers dozens of online discussion forums. If you're stuck on something, search the Apple discussion boards for advice. If you can't find an existing post that helps with your problem, go ahead and post a question.

MacScripter BBS

http://macscripter.net/

Although the MacScripter BBS is primarily an AppleScript forum, it does have an Automator category, which can be an excellent resource for getting expert Automator advice.

MAILING LISTS AND FORUMS

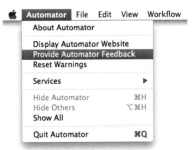

Figure 12.7 Choose Automator > Provide Automator Feedback to send Apple your input about Automator.

Figure 12.8 Use Apple's feedback webpage to let Apple know about bugs you encounter and features you'd like to see.

Sending Feedback to Apple

Apple values customer input and takes it into consideration when updating its software. Please let Apple know if you encounter any problems with Automator or if you have suggestions for features or actions you'd like to see. You never know; your suggestions just might make it into a future Automator release.

To provide Automator feedback:

1. Choose Automator > Provide Automator Feedback (**Figure 12.7**).

   Automator's feedback webpage opens in your web browser.

2. Enter your comments, and click Send Feedback (**Figure 12.8**).

Apple won't respond to your input directly. Rest assured, however, that your input is entered safely into Apple's database and will be taken into consideration.

✔ Tip

- You can provide feedback about most Apple products via Apple's website at www.apple.com/feedback.

Automator for Mac OS X 10.6 Snow Leopard: Visual QuickStart Guide Companion Website and Bonus Content

www.peachpit.com/vqs/automator-snow-leopard

Remember, there's even more to learn. Don't forget to visit this book's companion Website to register your book (see instructions in the Introduction) and gain access to the following bonus chapters:

◆ **Bonus Chapter 13, Workflow Starting Points:** Learn how to get started building workflows that process files and folders, music and audio, photos and images, movies, text, and more.

◆ **Bonus Chapter 14, Building Advanced Workflows:** Find out how AppleScript and UNIX can be used to create more robust and powerful Automator workflows.

◆ **Bonus Appendix B, Example Workflows:** Step-by-step instructions walk you through the creation of workflows that backup your Safari data, make dated subfolders, and clean up your desktop.

◆ **Bonus Appendix C, Developer Resources:** Learn where to go next if you want to begin writing your own custom Automator actions.

There's even more great content available online. You can find downloadable versions of the example workflows discussed throughout the book, as well as any extra information that may be added in the future.

COMPANION WEBSITE AND BONUS CONTENT

GLOSSARY

This glossary serves as a quick reference guide for many key Automator terms. Additional terms are explained within the text of *Automator for Mac OS X 10.6 Snow Leopard: Visual QuickStart Guide*. Please consult the Index if you are unable to locate a specific term.

◆ **Action.** An action is a building block within Automator. Each action is responsible for performing a single, specific automated task, and actions are placed together in sequence to form a workflow. Most actions have modifiable settings, allowing you to specify how they should behave when run within a workflow.

◆ **Application.** A workflow that is saved as an Application behaves like any other Mac OS X application. Double-click the Application to launch and run it, add it to your Dock, configure it as a login item, and more. Applications are drag and droppable. They pass any dropped items as input to the first action in the workflow for processing.

◆ **Folder Action.** An Automator workflow can be saved as a Folder Action and attached to a specified folder. When items are placed in the attached folder, the workflow runs and the newly added items are passed to the workflow for processing.

◆ **iCal Alarm.** A workflow saved as an iCal Alarm is attached to an iCal event and runs using an Open File alarm. Workflows of this nature can be scheduled to run during downtime or on a repeating schedule.

◆ **Image Capture Plugin.** An Image Capture Plugin is a workflow that can be run by the Image Capture application as photos are downloaded from a digital camera.

◆ **Input.** Most actions in Automator accept information from the previous action in the workflow as input. This information is generally processed by the action when the workflow runs. The type of input accepted by an action depends on the task the action performs. In some actions, input can be ignored.

◆ **Library.** The list of installed actions and variables, organized into categories, is known as Automator's Library. The Library is displayed along the left side of every workflow window, although it may be hidden from view, if desired.

◆ **Log.** Automator's log can be displayed at the bottom of a workflow window. When a workflow runs, the log provides a list of the events performed by the workflow, including any actions that have run, their duration, and a list of any errors that may have occurred.

◆ **Output.** Information that an action passes to the next phase of a workflow is known as the action's output (see Result).

◆ **Plugin.** Automator workflows can be built and saved as plugins for certain applications and processes in Mac OS X, including iCal, Image Capture, the Print system, and the system-wide Services architecture. Plugins offer a way to more tightly integrate Automator workflows into a daily routine without launching Automator.

◆ **Print Plugin.** Print Plugins appear in the PDF pop-up menu at the bottom of the Mac OS X Print window. While printing in any application, choose the workflow to print the current document to PDF format and pass it as input to the workflow for processing.

◆ **Recording.** Automator offers the ability to record manual tasks, such as mouse clicks and key presses. Recorded events are inserted into a workflow in the form of a Watch Me Do action. When the workflow runs, the recorded events are played back as part of the workflow.

◆ **Result.** Information an action passes to the next phase of a workflow is known as the action's result or output. The type of result an action produces varies depending on the function of the action. Typically, an action's result is passed to the next action in the workflow (which receives it as input) for further processing.

◆ **Script menu.** Mac OS X includes a system-wide script menu, which provides quick access to AppleScripts and Automator workflows from within any application. By default, the Script menu is disabled. It can be enabled via the AppleScript Editor application found in /Applications/Utilities.

◆ **Service.** Mac OS X's Services architecture offers a way for applications to share useful features with other applications. Automator workflows can be saved as Services, allowing them to be run within specified applications via the menu bar and sometimes from contextual menus and other locations. Service workflows can be configured to process selected input, such as text, URLs, image files, and more. When processing selected text, they can also be set to replace the text with processed text output by the workflow.

◆ **Timeout.** The amount of time allowed for a recorded manual event (within the Watch Me Do action) to be performed when run within an Automator workflow is known as a timeout. By default, recorded events are given a timeout of two seconds. This can be increased or decreased for recorded events on an individual basis, if desired.

◆ **Variable.** Variables provide a way to store and retrieve values as a workflow runs. A number of predefined variables are available, allowing a workflow to retrieve and use such dynamic information as the current time, current date, current user, system version, and more. Custom variables can also be used to store and retrieve action results, text, and more. Variables are new to Automator in Leopard.

◆ **Workflow.** A series of Automator actions that run in sequence to perform a set of automated tasks.

◆ **Workflow file.** A workflow saved as a file that can be opened and run within Automator. Some applications and processes, such as the Script menu, also provide mechanisms for running Automator workflow files.

◆ **Watch Me Do.** Used to insert recorded events into a workflow (see Recording).

WORKFLOW CREATION STEP-BY-STEP GUIDE

1. Determine the job you want to automate. Look for repetitive and time-consuming tasks you do on a regular basis.

2. List the steps needed to accomplish the job. You can do this in your head or as a written outline. Try to associate each step with an action in Automator.

3. Determine how you want to run the workflow. For example, do you want to run it within Automator, externally as an application, within another application to process selected text, and so forth?

4. Based on how you want to run the workflow, use Automator's template selection panel to create a new Workflow, Application, Service, Folder Action, Print Plugin, iCal Alarm, or Image Capture Plugin.

5. Certain types of workflows, such as Services and Folder Actions, provide configuration options in a header above the workflow area. Configure these workflow options, if applicable.

continues on next page

6. Locate the necessary actions in the Library list, and drag them to your workflow. To locate actions, try clicking through the different categories or entering keywords into the Library list's search field. If you can't find an action to accomplish a task, look online for a third-party action that can help.

7. Configure any action settings. To configure an action's settings at runtime, enable the "Show this action when the workflow runs" option (if available).

8. Determine whether any variables are necessary for your workflow to function. If so, insert them into the workflow and configure them.

9. Test the workflow by running it within Automator.

10. Check the status area and workflow log for errors. If errors occurred, troubleshoot and resolve them. Check action results to make sure the correct information is being passed through the workflow.

11. Save the workflow.

12. Run the workflow and become more efficient.

INDEX

INDEX

INDEX